Flowers
for
Weddings

Photography by Jeremy Whitaker MSIA

Flowers for Weddings

Pamela McNicol

B. T. Batsford Ltd, London

To Martin, Graham and Nick

© Pamela McNicol 1991
First published 1991
Reprinted 1992
Paperback edition 1995

ISBN 0 7134 7935 3
Typeset by Tradespools Limited, Frome, Somerset
and printed in Hong Kong
for the publishers
B. T. Batsford Ltd
4 Fitzhardinge Street
London W1H 0AH

Contents

Acknowledgements

I was delighted when Jill Findlay and Evelyn Mercer agreed to join me in producing a book on wedding flowers. I have the greatest admiration for their flower arranging, their ingenuity and their artistic ability to create a masterpiece whilst enjoying themselves at the same time. Surely we have done just that, for we have travelled to many interesting and very pleasant venues, we have been hosted by the most charming people and we have, indeed, had immense pleasure in producing the flower arrangements for this book.

We are all agreed that we were extremely lucky to acquire the services of Jeremy Whitaker as our photographer. His talents are outstanding and he pays meticulous attention to detail. His patience and tolerance of the idiosyncrasies of three flower arrangers must be greatly admired, and dare I hope that he has enjoyed it too.

Jill Findlay lives in Wokingham, Berkshire and has been a member of Maidenhead Flower Club for many years. She became Chairman and President of the Berks, Bucks & Oxon Area of NAFAS and held two national appointments as RHS Co-ordinator and Overseas Affiliates Chairman. During the formative years of the World Association of Flower Arrangers she served on the administrative committee whilst Britain was the first host country.

She was one of the three designers for the flower festival in Westminster Abbey in 1981 and has since been involved in the annual Commonwealth Service and the Royal Wedding in 1986. Her husband, Graham, was responsible for most of the mechanics used for the Royal Wedding, which are pictured in Chapter Eight. She has also travelled extensively, demonstrating flower arranging both at home and abroad.

Evelyn Mercer was born in the county of Kent and became involved in flower arranging towards the end of the 1950s when she joined the Sevenoaks Flower Club, later becoming its chairman. She was Chairman of the Kent area of NAFAS and is currently President of NAFAS. She has designed flower festivals in several stately homes, including Walmer Castle, Leeds Castle and Rochester Cathedral. She was a member of the NAFAS team for the Royal Wedding in 1986.

Evelyn qualified as a London and South East of England Registered Blue Badge guide and specializes in garden tours. By invitation of the Herbal Society of America she has lectured in several cities in Ohio and Connecticut.

Many other people have contributed so much to the compiling of this book. They have opened their homes to us, allowed us to invade them with flower boxes, cameras, lighting leads and all the paraphernalia which we seem to carry with us. We have occupied churches (and left them with flowers for the services that followed) and have appreciated the use of the wonderful settings of Eton College Chapel, Fishmongers Hall in London and Hever Castle in Kent.

We also give special thanks to Mary Newnes, Past President of NAFAS, who has spent many hours correcting plant names, and to Julia Clements OBE, VMH, Life Vice President of NAFAS, who has kindly written the Foreword to this book.

Finally, this book could not have been done without the help of the following. Thanks to: The Provost, Eton College; The Rev. J. Bundock, St Alban's Church, Hindhead; The Rev R. A. Ewbank, St Mary's Church, Bramshott; The Rev. W. J. Meyer, St Luke's Church, Grayshott; The Rev. W. M. Powell, St Francis' Church, Headley Down and All Saints' Church, Headley; The Rev. J. Song, St John's Church, St John's, Woking; Carter & Son (Thatcham) Ltd, Reading; The Management Committee, Grayshott Village Hall; Fishmongers Company, London; Hever Castle Ltd, Nr. Edenbridge, Kent; Captain & Mrs R. Hart; Mr & Mrs G. F. Kennedy; Mrs M. MacGeorge; Mr & Mrs R. Pilkington; Mr & Mrs A Rawcliffe; Mr & Mrs J. Sykes; Major & Mrs J. Whitaker; Mrs E. Ross (Bride); Mrs J. Scoon (Bride); Mrs Nicola McGutin (Bride); Camilla Whitaker (Bridesmaid); Peter McNicol (Page); David Longman; Anne Plowden; Beryl Greenslade; Rosamond Wills; Classic Cakes, Gosport; Brian Howard, Marley Flowers; and Louise Findlay.

Pictures of the Royal Wedding flowers are by courtesy of Syndication International; Peter Chivers; and Roy Smith.

Foreword

A WEDDING! Everyone loves a wedding. Whether you are a guest or one of the family or the radiant bride herself, there is no greater way of expressing the joy a wedding brings than with beautiful flowers.

But this book is about more than flowers, important as they are, for it covers every aspect of a wedding, whether simple or grand. Not the smallest detail is missed. No bride or those organizing a wedding need ever worry again, for this book says it all — even warning the groom about standing over a grille down which the ring might inadvertently be dropped.

At first I thought of referring to individual chapters, but then found that each one makes essential reading. However, I feel I must mention the chapter on the flowers for the Royal Wedding for they were a great work of floral art. Who but Pam McNicol, with her warm and generous nature, could have invoked the best out of the team that worked so enthusiastically with her on that great occasion? Her talent with flowers, as well as with a pen in her drawings, is well represented here.

This book is a *must* for everyone concerned with a wedding, from the smallest bit player to the star herself, and I wish it the great success I know it will enjoy.

Julia Clements, OBE, VMH
Chelsea, London

Introduction

I HAVE tried to provide a wide variety of information in this book which will be of interest to both experienced and potential flower arrangers. I hope readers will enjoy the quaint customs and traditions about which I have written in Chapter One. The guidelines for arranging wedding flowers, also to be found in the first chapter, were carefully thought out and are the result of many years experience of meeting brides, their mothers, vicars, hoteliers and marquee contractors, and assessing their wishes. Once decisions have been made the flower arranger's part in the proceedings can be carried out smoothly, with maximum ease and satisfaction. I hope that experienced flower arrangers will be able to relate our photographs to the diagrams of the mechanics used, and will understand how the arrangements have been done.

The chapter for beginners is to help those readers who are interested to know just 'how it is done'. Describing flower arranging by numbers seems to be very basic and could well produce the somewhat crude result found in a picture that has been painted by numbers. However, I would like to think that these simple directions give beginners a reasonable basis from which to develop their artistic ideas.

I have described the flowers for the Duke and Duchess of York's wedding in Westminster Abbey in 1986 in detail because, since that event, I have shown slides of these flower arrangements and lectured on their planning throughout this country and abroad, and it is these details that audiences have found interesting. Here, for the first time, they have been recorded on paper and show what a great achievement it was for the National Association of Flower Arrangement Societies.

To learn the art of floristry it is necessary to take a course at a school of floristry or study a book specifically on the subject. However, I am delighted that David Longman of Longmans Florists, London, who is currently the Master of the Worshipful Company of Gardeners, has agreed to write his thoughts on wedding bouquets and I include his chapter with great pleasure. I welcome his descriptions of the royal bouquets, for which his firm has been responsible since 1947.

Our suggestions for keepsakes from a wedding day are highlighted by Anne Plowden's section in Chapter Ten. I am most grateful to her, and also to Beryl Greenslade for providing us with the wedding plaque.

My final chapter on anniversaries is designed for nostalgia and includes, briefly, a few ideas for celebratory parties.

CHAPTER ONE

Flowers for weddings

IT IS interesting to note that, despite the current pace of life, 'a wedding' is as newsworthy as ever. Announcements and photographs of happy couples from all walks of life abound in local and national newspapers, glossy magazines and other publications. The bride may not be wearing a veil to cover her maidenly blushes, as in Victorian times when it was first introduced, but she does make a pretty picture, which all but the hardest of hearts amongst the guests cannot fail to admire — perhaps reminiscing themselves on their own nuptials, be they one or fifty years previously. Many ingredients go towards a happy wedding day, and although none should depend on the sun shining, this is always an added bonus.

One of the most important contributions to the atmosphere of the event is the flowers and it is by no means the most lavish display that proves the most successful. Thought, care and attention, coupled with an eye for pinpointing the interesting features of a venue, can often achieve quite a simple and effective result. The range of decorations are numerous and basic ideas may be adapted to suit any time of the year.

Good Luck

In this book we plan to set the scene for a variety of weddings and to show how flowers can reflect the simplicity of a village church or the grandeur of a cathedral; how they can enhance the austerity of a registry office or add a touch of glamour to a village hall. Brides may leave their cottage homes or their castles, in off-the-peg dresses or designer creations. Their flowers may be simple and countrified or exotic and worldly and they will plan their weddings in all seasons of the year. Behind every plan is the desire for this to be the 'day of days', for it is invariably the most important of all family events.

Once upon a time

Throughout history customs and superstitions are credited with bringing good and bad luck, happiness, success, good health and even large families to a bride and bridegroom.

During the betrothal period young girls of poorer families wove smocks of linen for their grooms to wear on the wedding day, trimming the garment with an embroidered collar dyed according to the groom's trade, and this smock was worn later by the husband when seeking employment. The pre-nuptial days for the girls of wealthy families were spent embroidering sleeves and collars with gold thread and richly coloured jewels for their betrothed.

The word 'spinster' used in the marriage banns comes from the single woman spinning her future husband's garment. Morbidly, soon after marriage, the bride's first task was to weave shrouds for herself and her spouse!

Choosing a time of the year or even a day of the week on which it is considered propitious to marry can present a problem. An old rhyme suggests that one should:

> Marry on Monday for health,
> Tuesday for wealth
> Wednesday the best day of all,
> Thursday for crosses,
> Friday for losses
> And Saturday for no luck at all.

Yet the modern bride presumably dismisses this warning in favour of the practicality of a Saturday wedding, now by far the most popular day. Another saying suggests that: 'If you marry in May you'll rue the day'. When families think of a June wedding, how many people know the origin of this age-old preference? In fact, the ancient Romans believed that Juno, the goddess of marriage, would bring prosperity and happiness to all who wed in her month. The practical advantages of marrying in June were that the bride was likely to bear her first child in early spring, allowing her time to recover before the next harvest. This was borne out in an ancient Scottish proverb which proclaims that: 'A fool marries in Yule, for when the corn's to shear the bairn's to bear'.

Even in the old calendar June was a popular month for weddings because, with the end of Lent and the arrival of warmer weather, it was the time for removing winter apparel and enjoying the annual bath! Brides were expected to bath, but it was not considered so necessary for the groom.

In the sixteenth and seventeenth centuries girls in their teens married in pale green, which was a sign of fertility. A girl in her twenties, considered to be a mature age, wore a brown dress and it is thought that Shakespeare's daughter, who was an older bride, was married in black.

Confetti is less popular these days – at least with vicars

Before the last century, brides tended to wear their best dress and the colour chosen was thought to influence their life:

Married in white, she has chosen right
Married in blue, her love will be true
Married in yellow, she'll be ashamed of her fellow
Married in red, she'll wish herself dead
Married in black, she'll wish herself back
Married in grey, she'll travel far away
Married in pink, of you he'll always think
Married in green, she'll be ashamed to be seen.

The white wedding dress came over with the Hanoverians and was initially worn only by the very wealthy, but later became popular with young Victorian girls. Nowadays, traditional white, ivory or pale peach are the most usual choices.

The ancient Egyptians first wore gold wedding rings, believing that the unbroken circle of the ring symbolized eternity, and the reason for wearing one on the third finger of the left hand dates back to the time when the Romans thought that a nerve led directly from that finger to the heart.

The Victorian era gave us our most revered wedding tradition – 'something old, something new, something borrowed, something blue, and a silver sixpence in your shoe'. Something old signifies the bride's link with her past life and she may wear a piece of her mother's jewellery. Something new will more than likely be the dress; borrowed, the veil or head-dress; and blue is often a garter or an embroidered handkerchief. The touch of blue symbolizes faithfulness, whilst 'a silver sixpence in your shoe' ensures future wealth and, despite inflation, a 5p piece would doubtless be a satisfactory substitute.

Brides' dresses present problems too. I wonder how many couturiers of today inform their seamstresses that they should not whistle at work whilst a dress is being made, since whistling may call up evil spirits! Also, the bride ought not to wear her complete wedding outfit before she dresses on the day, nor should the bridegroom see his bride on her wedding morning.

Most wedding traditions seem to apply to the bride, but the groom also has his share. He should carry his bride over the threshold of their new home to ensure she does not stumble, which would bring bad luck – another custom accredited to the Romans. However, the couple may acquire some good luck if their carriage to or from the church is pulled by a grey horse, and it is even an advantage merely to pass one! And, of course, a black cat or grubby chimney sweep ensures a large supply of good fortune.

The peal of church bells not only makes the populace aware that the ceremony has taken place, but it is also supposed to scare away any evil forces which may be lurking nearby. The showering of confetti promises happiness and children, yet nowadays many clergymen strike a rather mundane note when, at the end of the service, they ask the congregation not to throw any confetti in the churchyard with the obvious intention of preserving its tidiness. This tradition is another which emanates from the

Romans, when nuts were thrown at weddings, and this led to the custom of a bride giving gifts of sugared almonds to her guests. Confetti first came to this country in the form of cereal grain and, thereafter, rice, as both were supposed to signify a bountiful harvest and contentment.

Throughout history rose petals have been used on many occasions and for a variety of reasons. Antony and Cleopatra floated down the Nile on a barge with a mattress of rose petals, and petals have been strewn in the paths of brides since the earliest recorded Roman times. Centuries later, in 1863, fresh rose petals were thrown in the path of Princess Alexandra when she arrived on the shores of Great Britain to marry the Prince of Wales. Today confetti may be bought in the form of pale pink tissue paper rose petals.

One Anglo-Saxon custom was that a bride's father handed one of his daughter's shoes to his new son-in-law, thus confirming the transference of responsibility. He, in turn, tapped his bride on the head with the shoe and then took it with him to the bridal chamber, placing it on his side of the bed as a symbol of his authority. Shoes also played a part in Victorian weddings when they were thrown after the departing couple and today, invariably, old boots are tied to the going-away car along with the razzmatazz of messages in lipstick and shaving cream, balloons and streamers.

The charming custom of a bride tossing her bouquet to her bridesmaids as she leaves finds less favour these days. There is a growing trend for preserving the bouquet in one of the several forms described later in this book, which provides a permanent reminder of the flowers carried on the wedding day.

We request the pleasure

Choosing the date is, of course, number one priority. It must be convenient to the families of both bride and groom, and an early check should be made as to whether the vicar or priest in charge of the church is available to perform the service.

Nowadays weddings in Lent or Advent may take place, but it is possible that the church will not allow flowers or, if they do, they may have to be

Goodbye and have a good time!

Will I be the next bride?

removed before the services on the following Sunday. Careful consideration should be given to winter weddings, when weather conditions may be adverse, making travel difficult for guests, yet there has been snow in April and even a marquee in June has been known to be cold!

Once the date is fixed a guest list should be compiled. At times the wishes of the bride and groom have been overshadowed by everyone else's convictions that . . . 'so and so should be asked', 'we must invite . . .' and 'what about . . .?', and the intention of a small, family wedding soon sinks without trace. Whatever the outcome of these discussions, the invitations should be posted six weeks before the day and thereafter replies will be awaited eagerly. Many decisions must be taken as early as possible and seemingly endless arrangements made in the months leading up to the wedding.

Since the bride and groom have decided to be married in church, it is for them to consult the vicar on the order of service and to select the hymns and music for the ceremony. The venue for the reception must be chosen and caterers, photographer, flower arrangers and florist must be selected and booked. All are vital components of an occasion which will be long remembered. Other decisions may follow – who will be the best man, the bridesmaids or pages? Who will propose the health of the couple? Who will make the cake?

But the primary concern of this book is the flowers and so I shall begin by listing what has to be done to ensure that a bride has the kind of flowers she wants in the church, at the reception and in her home.

Things to do

The bride's mother and/or the bride should:

(1) Choose and confirm *who* will do the flowers.
(2) Arrange a meeting with the flower arranger to discuss requirements, design and colour scheme, providing a pattern of the bridesmaids' dresses.
(3) Inform the vicar as to who will be designing the flowers and tactfully establish his views on the placing of them in his church (this will chiefly concern the altar and the font).
(4) Contact the next most important person, the 'church flower lady', and ensure that the wedding is entered on her flower rota for the appropriate weekend.
(5) Enquire whether any other weddings are booked on the same day in the church and, if so, liaise with the respective brides' families with a view to sharing the flowers and their cost and, hopefully, to agree on a mutually suitable colour scheme.

The flower arranger should then:

(1) Contact the vicar and/or 'church flower lady' to enquire when the church is open and who holds the key.

(2) Ascertain from the vicar the timing of any special services, choir practices, etc. which might affect when the work can be done.

(3) Be prepared to accept that a funeral service may take place just when the flowers were to be arranged. There is little forward planning for a funeral in the church calendar.

(4) Locate the water tap and find out what equipment is in the church. The use of as many containers belonging to the church as possible makes the clearing up process much easier.

(5) It is helpful to know if there is a rubbish heap in the churchyard and, also, the whereabouts of brushes and dustpans.

Every flower arranger should bear these important points in mind when doing wedding flowers:

- Remember that it is a wedding and not a flower festival.
- The bride should be enhanced by flowers and *not* overshadowed by them.
- A few well-planned arrangements are preferable to numerous small ones on every ledge and in every alcove.
- Do not underrate the value of garden flowers and foliage as the perfect foil to more exotic flowers. A 'mound' of solid flowers is never as attractive as an arrangement which is framed by and interspersed with plenty of foliage.
- Never forget the saying 'belts and braces' when planning the mechanics for the flowers. A toppled arrangement, especially if it occurs as the bride arrives, is bound to suggest bad luck to someone in the congregation.

If the flower arranger is undecided on how much to spend she should, at an early stage, ask the vital question of the bride's mother. The answer will be – 'I can't afford much, but I want it to look nice'; or 'well ... do your best, don't stint'; or 'spend whatever is necessary'.

When the reception is held in a marquee the flower arranger will need the following information:

- Colour of the lining.
- How many poles are there? Is it a frame marquee without poles?
- Is there a covered way?
- Where will the entrance, receiving line and cake table be?
- When will the marquee be erected?

If the reception is to be held in a village hall or hotel the arranger will need to know:

- When will the room/rooms be available for decoration?
- Is there another booking before or after the wedding?

- If so, would the organisers of the event after the wedding like the flowers to remain and, possibly, contribute to their cost?

Flowers in the bride's home should be done to suit the social commitments of the family as it is preferable for them to be finished in time for any pre-wedding parties which may be planned.

Finally, an essential list for the bridegroom:

(1) He is responsible for the payment of the bride's and bridesmaids' bouquets, the ushers' buttonholes and any corsages which may be required. Doubtless his bride will choose the type of flowers she would prefer and a visit to the local florist should be made in good time so that the requirements are carefully booked into what might become 'a busy Saturday'.

(2) He should order and pay for the wedding cars.

(3) He will, no doubt, organize the honeymoon.

(4) He should choose small gifts to present to his best man and to the bridesmaids.

(5) He will buy the ring or rings.

Without this ring, I thee wed

CHAPTER TWO

Spring weddings

THE FIRST spring wedding took place in a tiny, country church which was originally nothing more than a wooden hut to which, at a later date, a modern chancel was added with a most unusual half-circular east window. An oak table with a plain wooden cross, hand carved by a parishioner, and the modern, low, silver candleholders, provided an altar. In early spring, florists' flowers are expensive and the new growth of garden foliage is difficult to condition, so the choice of flowers used was largely from gardens and the foliage was carefully selected for its lasting qualities. The soft colours of pale pink hyacinths and blossom blended with cream daffodils, while iris and tulips gave warmth and depth to otherwise light and airy arrangements.

The two 91 cm (36 in) arrangements on the windowsill, curving at the top to follow the line of the window, were done on metal stands (mechanics no. 24*, smaller version).

FOLIAGE
Acer platanoides (Norway maple)
Amelanchier laevis
Arum italicum 'Pictum'
cupressus
Euonymus fortunei radicans
  'Silver Queen'
Prunus laurocerasus (laurel)
Prunus laurocerasus 'Otto Luyken'
Viburnum tinus

FLOWERS
13 Narcissus 'Ice Follies'
 2 stems Helleborus niger
 7 Iris 'White Wedgewood'
 7 tulip 'White Parrot'

Note
*Throughout the book the mechanics used will be referred to by numbers & the instructions can be found in Chapter six.

Two square blocks of floral foam 12.7 × 12.7 cm (5 × 5 in), wrapped in thin polythene, were secured on the altar candlesticks by their central spike, and the candles, with four cocktail sticks fixed round their bases with clear adhesive tape, were inserted into the foam (mechanics no. 21).

For one candlestick:

FOLIAGE	FLOWERS
Buxus sempervirens (box)	2 stems cream spray carnation
cupressus (golden)	1 *Helleborus orientalis*
Hedera helix 'Marginata' (ivy)	2 *Helleborus foetidus*
Spiraea × *arguta* 'Bridal Wreath'	1 small pink hyacinth
	2 *Lilium* 'Sterling Star'

The large, flowing arrangement on the carpeted platform beneath the altar was in a round, flat basket fitted with a glass flan dish which contained one standard block of floral foam.

FOLIAGE	FLOWERS
Arum italicum 'Pictum'	3 stems cream spray carnation
cupressus (golden)	5 cream carnation
Hebe anomala (shrubby Veronica)	5 sprays pink and white cherry
Hedera helix 'Marginata' (ivy)	blossom
Lonicera nitida 'Baggesen's Gold' (box	6 *Euphorbia robbiae* (spurge)
honeysuckle)	5 *Helleborus orientalis*
Spiraea × *arguta* 'Bridal Wreath'	5 pale pink hyacinth
	7 *Iris* 'White Wedgewood'
	7 tulip 'White Parrot'

St Francis Church, Headley; altar

St Mary's Church, Bramshott; gateway

When planning the decorations in any church, it is especially welcoming to greet the guests with flowers at the entrance. A glimpse of the thirteenth-century church through the archway of flowers gave the guests a delightful welcome to this country wedding on a sunny, spring afternoon. Polythene parcels were tied round the wrought iron arch, and foliage and flowers were tucked in both sides so that the view was equally attractive when leaving the church as on arrival. Two plaques were tied to the base of the arch above the gate posts and hung down on each side.

Arch (mechanics no. 4)

FOLIAGE
cupressus (golden)
Hebe anomala (shrubby Veronica)
Ruta graveolens (rue)

FLOWERS
white spray carnations (split up)
feverfew flowers

Each plaque (mechanics no. 6b)

FOLIAGE
cupressus (golden)
Ligustrum ovalifolium 'Aureum' (golden
   privet)

FLOWERS
1 stem single white chrysanthemum
  (split up)
1 stem chrysanthemum 'White Spider'
  Gypsophila paniculata 'Bristol Fairy'
2 cream *Gerbera jamesonii*
  (Transvaal/Barbeton daisy)

Here, the alcoves in this ancient, country church porch lent themselves to small, hanging flower balls. Ribbon streamers that matched the flowers also complemented the colours worn by the bridesmaids.

For one ball (mechanics no. 11c)

FOLIAGE
Asparagus sprengeri (trailing house
   plant)
cupressus (golden)
Forsythia × *intermedia* 'Spectabilis'
Hebe anomala (shrubby veronica)
Hedera helix 'Glacier' (ivy)

FLOWERS
18 side shoots cream spray carnation
15 lemon jonquil narcissus

All Saints' Church, Headley; porch

Sides of arch
(mechanics no. 1a and 1b)

FOLIAGE
Buxus sempervirens (box)
cupressus (golden)

FLOWERS
10 stems lemon florist's spray
        chrysanthemum (split up)
20 lemon jonquil narcissus

Centre top of arch
(mechanics no. 8a)

FOLIAGE
Amelanchier laevis
Euonymus fortunei radicans 'Silver Queen'
Hedera helix 'Glacier' (ivy)
Spiraea × *arguta* 'Bridal Wreath'

FLOWERS
1 stem cream spray carnation
2 *Lilium* 'Sterling Star'

All Saints' Church, Headley; altar

There is a beautiful carved choir screen in the church, which we framed with a comparatively slim archway of flowers, affording a glimpse of a simple arrangement of lilies twisting round the altar cross.

This church catered for its congregation with care. There was an excellent sound system, one amplifier on each window which, though somewhat highlighted here, in reality blended with the stonework quite unobtrusively. The church was also aware of its flower arrangers' needs and constructions had been made for each sloping windowsill in the form of shelves which fitted existing hooks to provide neat platforms on which to put flower containers. This arrangement was made in a flat container with one block of floral foam taped, not only to the mechanics, but also round the shelf (mechanics no. 16a and 16b).

FOLIAGE
Amelanchier laevis
Camellia japonica
Hedera canariensis (ivy)
Spiraea × arguta 'Bridal Wreath'

FLOWERS
5 stems cream spray carnation
5 spray chrysanthemum 'Bonnie Jean'
5 *Iris* Dutch hybrid
3 *Lilium* 'Destiny'
5 *Lilium* 'Sterling Star'

All Saints' Church, Headley; window sill

24

A quite different and most unusual windowsill allowed the placements of flowers to flow from the higher level to the lower. The sills were level, so special mechanics were not required and two trays of floral foam were used to achieve this cascade effect.

FOLIAGE
Danae racemosa (ruscus)
Dryopteris filix-mas (male fern)
Hedera helix 'Marginata' (ivy)
Ligustrum ovalifolium 'Aureum' (golden privet)
Viburnum tinus 'Laurustinus'

FLOWERS
7 cream carnation
9 stems white spray carnation
7 stems single white chrysanthemum
5 stems chrysanthemum 'White Spider'
  Gypsophila paniculata 'Bristol Fairy'
  feverfew flowers
15 *Iris* 'White Wedgewood'
5 *Lilium* 'Sterling Star'
7 narcissus 'Passionale'
7 *Rosa* 'Jack Frost'
9 single white tulip

St Mary's Church, Bramshott; window sill

The pew ends were decorated with sprays of flowers arranged in florette cases, which were attached with string threaded through their handles. To ensure uniformity, each piece of string must be the same length. Particular care should be taken to cover the sides of the mechanics, since the overall effect will be viewed while walking up or down the aisle (mechanics no. 17c).

FOLIAGE
cupressus
erica (heather)
Hedera helix 'Aureavariegata' (ivy)
Lonicera nitida 'Baggesen's Gold' (box honeysuckle)

FLOWERS
3 stems cream spray carnation
1 chrysanthemum 'Bonnie Jean'
2 *Lilium* 'Sterling Star'
2 polyanthus

All Saints' Church, Headley; pew end

25

Columns of flowers each side of this simple altar made a pretty setting for a spring wedding. The church dates back to 1220 and the plain stone walls, the cream curtain and the gold and cream altar frontal complement each other perfectly. The glass in the windows behind was given in memory of the Canadian soldiers stationed in the area during the two world wars, and each province of Canada is named.

The flowers were arranged in metal stands and two extra trays of floral foam placed in front of the columns on the altar step allowed the flowers to curl round the corners of the altar and over the step (mechanics no. 24).

St Mary's Church, Bramshott; altar cross

For each column

FOLIAGE
Danae racemosa (ruscus)
Hebe 'Midsummer Glory'
Ligustrum ovalifolium 'Aureum' (golden privet)
Prunus laurocerasus (laurel)
Viburnum tinus 'Laurustinus'
Sorbus aria 'Lutescens'

FLOWERS
  7 cream carnation
  7 single white spray chrysanthemum
  7 stems chrysanthemum 'White Spider'
15 Iris 'White Wedgewood'
  7 *Lilium* 'Sterling Star'
  4 white *Matthiola* 'Brompton Strain' (stock)
     white cherry blossom

The close-up of the gold cross shows its beauty and that of the Mont Blanc lilies which, curling round its base, enhanced it whilst not overwhelming it. Three stems of lily and five *Arum italicum* leaves were used in a saucer of floral foam placed behind the cross.

St Mary's Church, Bramshott; altar

This beautiful country cottage was the venue for a small, informal wedding reception. The cake was set on a round table covered with a circular, nylon net cloth over a jersey underskirt. Two posies of flowers arranged in polythene parcels reflected the pale pink and peach colour scheme, which was carried through to the ribbons as well. The flowers on top of the cake were to scale with the small silver salt cellar in which they were arranged.

Cake table

FOLIAGE	FLOWERS
Heuchera	Anthriscus sylvestris (cow parsley/Queen Anne's lace)
Kalmia latifolia	
Pieris japonica 'Variegata'	petite white florist rose
Symphoricarpos orbiculatus 'Variegatus' (snowberry)	Rosa 'Perle d'Or'
Vinca major 'Elegantissima' (greater periwinkle)	

Two discreetly placed nails were fixed to the oak beam to hold the mechanics for the frame of flowers which decorated it. This avoided taking up the limited space of a small room, yet provided a spectacular display of flowers, as much above the heads of the guests as the height of the ceiling allowed. Mostly garden flowers were used and the lightness and airiness of the arrangement was enhanced by the use of cow parsley from the hedgerows (mechanics no. 2b and 8a).

Plaque

FOLIAGE	FLOWERS
Abeliophyllum distichum	Anthriscus sylvestris (cow parsley/ Queen Anne's lace)
cupressus (golden)	
Hedera helix 'Glacier' (ivy)	7 stems pink azalea
Kalmia latifolia	5 stems white spray carnation
Pieris japonica 'Variegata'	7 pink carnation
Weigela florida 'Variegata'	5 stems chrysanthemum 'Bonnie Jean' (split up)
	Tellima grandiflora

Cake table complemented by a plaque of flowers on an oak beam

A bride pauses momentarily on the landing of this imposing staircase. Behind her is a 1.5 m (5 ft) high arrangement in a large, shallow, copper preserving pan on the wide windowsill. The curving bannister of this section of the stairs was garlanded with flowers and the newel posts topped with saucers containing greenery and heads of white spray carnations. Plaques beneath these held sprays of foliage to give extra interest.

Windowsill

FOLIAGE
Danae racemosa (ruscus)
Hebe 'Midsummer Beauty'
Ligustrum ovalifolium 'Aureum' (golden privet)
Spiraea × *arguta* 'Bridal Wreath'
flowering Japanese cherry

FLOWERS
1 cream carnation
7 stems single white chrysanthemum
5 stems deep cream single chrysanthemum
13 stems chrysanthemum 'White Spider'
 Euphorbia robbiae (spurge)
20 *Iris* 'White Wedgewood'
9 *Lilium* dull peach
11 *Lilium* 'Sterling Star'
11 narcissus 'Passionale'
9 cream *Matthiola* 'Brompton Strain' (stock)

Garland (mechanics no. 4)

FOLIAGE
cupressus (golden)
Hebe anomala
Ruta graveolens (rue)

FLOWERS
white spray carnations (split up)
feverfew flowers

Plaques (mechanics no. 6b)

FOLIAGE
cupressus (golden)
Ligustrum ovalifolium 'Aureum' (golden privet)

FLOWERS
3 stems single white chrysanthemum (split up)
1 stem chrysanthemum 'White Spider'
 Euphorbia robbiae (spurge)
 Gypsophila paniculata 'Bristol Fairy'
9 *Rosa* 'Jack Frost'

A staircase fit for a bride

A glamorous arrangement for a wedding in a reception room at Fishmongers Hall in London is pictured here, and one can enjoy the reflections in the mirror behind the flowers on the mantelpiece.

A close-up of these flowers is seen in the photograph opposite and shows the advantage of a single, large and impressive arrangement in a room such as this. The container was a plastic trough containing three blocks of floral foam taped together. It was well weighted at the back, as the width of the mantelpiece meant that most of the flowers were placed towards the front of the container. Care was taken to fill the back of the arrangement with foliage since it would be reflected in the mirror.

Fishmongers Hall; mantelpiece

FOLIAGE

Asparagus sprengeri
Danae racemosa (ruscus)
Escallonia 'Crimson Spire'
Eucalyptus gunnii (gum tree)
Rosmarinus officinalis (rosemary)
Senecio greyi

FLOWERS

 5 pink *Alstroemeria* 'Ligtu Hybrids' (Peruvian lily)
 5 pink spray carnation
 5 white carnation
 9 pink carnation
 5 orange carnation
 3 pale pink single spray chrysanthemum
10 mid-pink single spray chrysanthemum
 9 peach single spray chrysanthemum
 5 pink gladioli
 5 pink hydrangea heads
 5 *Lilium* 'Love's Dream'
 4 *Lilium* 'Longiflorum'
10 *Rosa* 'Sonia'
10 pink tulip

Fishmongers Hall; mantelpiece close-up

Increasingly, more and more types of flowers are available at all times of the year and a visit to a flower market shows that the seasons barely seem to exist. One finds buckets of delphiniums and peonies in early spring and roses throughout the year. Spray chrysanthemums, certainly, are obtainable in every season, though I prefer to use the single daisy type in spring and summer and save the double ones for autumn and winter.

Spring weddings present the greatest problem for finding mature foliage, and one hopes that any wedding might manage to time itself for the opening of the beautiful silvery green leaves of whitebeam which, although difficult to condition in its early stages, becomes a magnificent standby as the leaves mature. The curving branches seem to be designed especially for flower arranging as, indeed, do many other types of spring foliage and flowering shrubs.

CHAPTER THREE

Summer weddings

'THINK PINK', we are told, and the first summer bride did just that. Her dress was a soft oyster shade and her little bridesmaid, seen reflected in the swimming pool and tentatively dipping her flower ball in the water, wore a short dress with matching hair band in beautiful, soft pink Thai silk. The two adult attendants wore classically simple dresses in a similar colour. The flowers throughout the church, marquee and house were in cream and shades of pink, and the best man and ushers wore buttonholes of pink carnations. Guests wandered around the garden and the beautiful swimming pool and enjoyed the flowers arranged on a peach-coloured pedestal (mechanics no. 27a).

FOLIAGE

Dryopteris filix-mas (male fern)
Philadelphus 'Virginal' (mock orange)
Sorbus aria (whitebeam)
Spiraea thunbergii
Tilia × europaea (lime stripped of its leaves)

FLOWERS

  3 *Digitalis purpurea* 'Alba' (foxglove)
  9 pink carnation
  7 cream carnation
  7 *Lavatera olbia* 'Rosea'
  5 *Lilium* 'Longiflorum'
13 *Paeonia lactiflora* pale pink (peony)

The arrangement on the edge of the pool used similar flowers and foliage, and was done in a shallow container using one block of floral foam which had been secured with tape.

Summer weddings . . . and one thinks of long, hazy days of sunshine, marquee sides rolled up, vistas of beautifully tended gardens and guests with clicking cameras wandering amongst flower beds that have been meticulously weeded for the occasion. In reality it is not always quite like that; often, muddy covered ways lead to dripping marquees and flapping canvas mars the speeches. Nevertheless, under this summer section we will describe the decoration of marquees, which needs careful consideration when planning the flowers.

Sometimes the site for a marquee is such that a tree has to be included within it. This can be put to good use and, indeed, may become a feature in the decoration. At my own daughter's wedding we had no choice but to erect the marquee on a part of the garden where there was a rather rare and beautifully-shaped Japanese maple. Far from 'getting in the way', I used its branches to carry flowers, lashing sections of floral foam wrapped in thin polythene to them and arranging dainty flowers and foliage along the lines of the tree. It was then floodlit from below, making a dramatic centrepiece and a talking point amongst the guests.

Whilst preparing for another wedding I remember the bride's mother worrying that there would be a large and empty dovecot right in the middle of the marquee. What a wonderful centrepiece this turned out to be. Containers of floral foam were fixed in each hole of the cot and sprays of blossom, trailing foliage and flowers cascaded in all directions. Instead of being an embarrassment to the hostess, the dovecot, she told me afterwards, had been mentioned in every single thank-you letter she received and, after a while, she had begun to wonder if anyone had noticed the bride!

Temptation by a pool

The golden rule for the decoration of marquees is that the flowers should be sited well above the guests' heads. Pedestals placed round the edges of a marquee are not always shown to their best advantage, since the roof normally sweeps down to comparatively low sides and the flowers would be barely visible when the marquee was full of guests.

In a traditional marquee the poles are the first thing to consider, and it will depend upon the size of the marquee as to whether all or alternate ones are decorated. Everyone has ideas for poles and we have chosen several methods, all of which can be varied in size to suit the venue.

The first is the more traditional ring of flowers arranged in three florettes. The flowers were placed loosely with plenty of foliage and were encircled with gypsophila to give a dainty effect (mechanics no. 6a).

The ring can be made larger by using bigger pieces of floral foam in shallow trays fixed round the pole in the same way, and with longer stems of flowers and foliage (mechanics no. 8b). A pair of plastic garden flower baskets can also be used to great effect by wiring or taping them together and stapling to either side of the pole (mechanics no. 10).

FOLIAGE
Philadelphus coronarius 'Variegatus' (mock orange)
Kalmia latifolia (American laurel)
cupressus
Euonymus fortunei radicans 'Silver Queen'
Tilia × europaea (lime stripped of its leaves)

FLOWERS
Alchemilla mollis (lady's mantle)
Alstroemeria 'Regina' (Peruvian lily)
Gypsophila paniculata 'Bristol Fairy'
Lathyrus odorata (sweet pea)
Paeonia lactiflora (peony)
Rosa 'Blessings' 'Royal Romance'

Pink marquee

Flowers should be above the guests' heads

Flowers around a pole

The pole in the yellow and white striped marquee illustrates the second method of decoration. Here the flowers curl around the pole by means of a spiral of plastic netting enclosing moss and pieces of floral foam. This is fixed firstly at a height which can be comfortably reached from the ground for arranging and, when complete, raised to the correct height and any odd spaces filled with flowers and foliage (mechanics no. 3a).

FOLIAGE	FLOWERS
cupressus	*Alchemilla mollis* (lady's mantle)
Deutzia × magnifica	13 stems white spray chrysanthemum
Euonymus fortunei radicans 'Silver Queen'	11 white *Gerbera jamesonii* (Transvaal/ Barbeton daisy)
Ligustrum sinense 'Variegatum' (privet)	*Gypsophila paniculata* 'Bristol Fairy'
Philadelphus 'Belle Etoile' (mock orange)	9 *Lilium* 'Sterling Star'
Sorbaria aitchisonii (false spiraea)	5 *Paeonia lactifolia* white (peony)
	Rosa 'Bridal Pink'

Another summer wedding provided a more unusual colour scheme which stemmed from the choice of marquee. No soft frills or dainty colours but smart, eyecatching blue and white stripes. The circular, framed marquee, without poles, gave the perfect setting for a ring of flowers hoisted up to the centre of the roof. Many marquee firms will provide ropes and pulleys for suspending such arrangements as this circle of flowers. Flower balls are also lifted into position in this way, and the method for arranging them is described in the chapter on flowers for the Royal Wedding.

Both the ring of flowers and the flower ball, complete with soaked floral foam and plant material, can be very heavy, and care must be taken to ensure that the pulley and rope are strong enough to take the strain. Most marine rope is adequate for this purpose (mechanics no. 9).

An added attraction resulted quite by chance at the evening party when the disco's glass ball, placed in the centre of our flower ring, reflected the bright lights as it turned, producing a quite magical effect.

FOLIAGE
Choisya ternata (Mexican orange blossom)
cupressus (golden)
Hebe anomala (shrubby veronica)
Hedera colchica 'Dentata' (ivy)
hosta (plantain lily)
Ligustrum ovalifolium 'Aureum' (golden privet)

FLOWERS
12 blue agapanthus
15 white *Gerbera jamesonii* (Transvaal/ Barbeton daisy)
15 heads blue hydrangea
24 *Iris* 'Ideal'
20 *Lilium* 'Connecticut King'
50 *Scabiosa caucasica* (scabious)

Blue marquee; ring of flowers

An archway of flowers

There should always be a pleasing and welcoming decoration to a marquee and plaques of flowers attached each side of the entrance, topiary trees or an archway of flowers outlining the doorway are all suitable. There are usually metal struts to which mechanics can be fixed, and the archway pictured here clearly shows how effective it can be when an entrance is framed with flowers, providing an eyecatching part of the marquee decoration as a whole. The foliage and flowers faced both ways and could be appreciated from either direction. The pale cream colouring darkened to pale apricot as it reached the larger base arrangements, which were in washing up bowls.

Looking down the covered passageway a pair of topiary trees can be seen (mechanics no. 14) – two of a series of trees, arranged with similar plant material to the arch (mechanics no. 3b), at the entrance to the marquee.

Archway

FOLIAGE
Buxus sempervirens (box)
cupressus
Hebe anomala
Hebe 'Midsummer Beauty'
Hedera helix 'Cristata'
Lonicera nitida 'Baggesen's Gold'
Pieris japonica
Prunus lusitanica 'Portugal laurel'

FLOWERS
12 cream carnation
15 stems single lemon chrysanthemum
    (split up)
 8 stems single dull peach
    chrysanthemum
15 stems chrysanthemum 'White Spider'
   Euphorbia robbiae (spurge)
   Gypsophila paniculata 'Bristol Fairy'
10 *Lilium* 'Mont Blanc'
10 *Lilium* 'Sterling Star'
 6 *Rosa* 'Champagne'

This stand carries a 'birdcage' of flowers arranged in a shallow container.

Birdcage

FOLIAGE
Deutzia × magnifica
Dryopteris filix-mas (male fern)
Ligustrum sinense 'Variegatum' (privet)
Tilia × europaea (lime stripped of its
  leaves)

FLOWERS
 5 cream carnation
 3 stems chrysanthemum 'Bonnie Jean'
 3 stems chrysanthemum 'White Spider'

Most receptions, whether they are in marquees, hotels or village halls, try to provide some tables at which guests may sit and these will require small and simple table centres. They are normally done in a saucer containing a small block of floral foam approximately 10 × 10 cm (4 × 4 ins). Fewer flowers than are pictured here may be used and a pretty effect can also be achieved by using a basis of small, mixed foliage (e.g. cupressus, heather, box, etc.) and a few heads of spray carnations and spray chrysanthemums interspersed with small pieces of gypsophila. Tiny bows of ribbon wired to short lengths of stub wire may be added and, should the wedding party continue into the evening, a candle may be inserted in the centre of the arrangement (mechanics no. 21).

FOLIAGE
Asparagus sprengeri
Hedera helix 'Marginata' (ivy)

FLOWERS
5 peach spray carnation
3 cream chrysanthemum 'White Spider'
2 peach single spray chrysanthemum *Gypsophila paniculata* 'Bristol Fairy'
2 *Lilium* 'Mont Blanc'
5 yellow jonquil narcissus
3 pink mini orchid
3 yellow florist's rose

1 × 25 cm (10 in) high peach-coloured candle

Table centre

Whilst caterers, on the whole, jealously guard their table space, there should always be some kind of decoration on the buffet table. One large arrangement is often best with, possibly, the front and sides of the table garlanded.

Here, floral foam was fitted into a silver container which was raised on a trivet covered with material in the centre of the table. Flowers in flat trays flowed over the corners of the table and tiny parcels of floral foam wrapped in thin polythene were pinned to the cloth to provide posies at each side of the central arrangement.

Centre Arrangement

FOLIAGE
Asparagus plumosus (asparagus fern)
Hedera helix 'Glacier' (ivy)
Kalmia latifolia (American laurel)
Philadelphus microphyllus (mock orange)
Tilia × europaea (lime stripped of its leaves)
Vinca major (periwinkle)

FLOWERS
Alchemilla mollis (lady's mantle)
Alstroemeria 'Ligtu Hybrids' (Peruvian lily)
7 pale pink carnation
Gypsophila paniculata 'Bristol Fairy'
3 hosta flowers (plantain lily)
Lavatera olbia 'Rosea' (mallow)
Lathyrus odorata (sweet pea)
Lilium 'Sterling Star'
7 Rosa 'Bridal Pink'
Syringa microphylla (lilac)

Florettes

FOLIAGE
Asparagus plumosus (asparagus fern)
Tilia × europaea (lime stripped of its leaves)

FLOWERS
Alchemilla mollis (lady's mantle)
spray carnations
Lathyrus odorata (sweet pea)
Lilium 'Sterling Star'

Two focal points are required in the decoration of a marquee: one should be adjacent to the receiving line and the other well placed to complement the bride and bridegroom as they cut the cake. Pictured in the pink marquee is a striking, three-tiered arrangement which would be equally suitable in either position (mechanics no. 23).

Three-tiered stand

FOLIAGE
Dryopteris filix-mas (male fern)
Kalmia latifolia (American laurel)
Philadelphus microphyllus (mock orange)
Polygonatum multiflorum (Solomon's seal)
Sorbaria aitchisonii (false spiraea)
Vinca major (periwinkle)

FLOWERS
Alchemilla mollis (lady's mantle)
Alstroemeria 'Ligtu Hybrids' (Peruvian lily)
spray carnations
Gypsophila paniculata 'Bristol Fairy'
Lathyrus odorata (sweet pea)
Lavatera olbia 'Rosea' (mallow)
Paeonia lactiflora pale pink (peony)

Buffet table

Torchère

FOLIAGE
cupressus (golden)
Megasea
Pinus lambertiana (sugar pine)
rhododendron
Taxus baccata 'Repens Aurea' (yew)
Viburnum
Euphorbia 'Kwikzilver' (white)

FLOWERS
cream spray carnations
cream carnations
spray chrysanthemum:
 'Cassa'
 'Daymark'
 'Refour'
cream gerbera
Freesia × *hybrid*

Flower Ball

FOLIAGE
cupressus (golden)
Hebe anomala
Hedera helix 'Silver Queen' (*ivy*)
Pinus lambertiana (sugar pine)

FLOWERS
cream spray carnations
spray chrysanthemum: 'Daymark'
Freesia × *hybrid*

Blue, yellow and white flowers decorate this porch and are arranged in a pair of two-tiered stands (mechanics no. 13) on either side of the inner door. We catch a glimpse of a small pedestal of flowers with a lower placement which greeted guests as they entered the church (mechanics no. 26).

For one stand

FOLIAGE
Choisya ternata (Mexican orange blossom)
cupressus (golden)
Foeniculum vulgare (fennel)
hosta (plantain lily)
Lonicera nitida 'Baggesen's Gold'
Ribes sanguineum (flowering currant)
Taxus baccata 'Repens Aurea' (yew)

FLOWERS
Aster ericoides 'Monte Casino'
 (Michaelmas daisy)
Alchemilla mollis (lady's mantle)
4 blue agapanthus
5 blue delphiniums
Gypsophila paniculata 'Bristol Fairy'
5 gold carnations
3 cream carnations
3 single cream spray chrysanthemum
Centaurea cyanus (cornflower)
Nigella damascena (love-in-a-mist)

A pair of the same metal torchères (mechanics no. 26) is seen decorating the porch of another church. Used slightly differently, they are each standing on a metal trivet to raise them from the ground and the lower arrangements are much larger. Out of the top a cascade of lovely bear grass falls like a green fountain amongst the flowers. A flower ball is suspended in the centre of the doorway (mechanics no. 11c) and inside the porch beneath an unusual modern engraved glass window a long, low arrangement rises approximately 60 cm (24 in).

St John's Church, Woking; porch

The aisle along which this bride processed to meet her bridegroom is decorated with plaques on the end of each pew. Personal taste dictates whether every or alternate pews are decorated, but the overall effect should be balanced (mechanics no. 17b).

A pair of three-tiered arrangements was placed each side of the west end of the aisle (mechanics no. 25a) and a single, large pedestal can be seen on the right of the chancel (mechanics no. 27a). The font in this Victorian church was moved some years ago and placed immediately in front of the altar; an unusual setting, but the dainty ring of flowers circling its top made another feature of interest to the overall aspect. A simple arrangement of five stems of Longiflorum lilies complemented the altar cross.

Pew End (quantity for one)

FOLIAGE	FLOWERS
cupressus (golden)	1 *Lilium* 'Sterling Star'
Hedera helix 'Silver Queen' (ivy)	florets from stems of florist's spray
Vinca major (periwinkle)	chrysanthemum split up:
	'Cassa'
	'Daymark'
	'Snowdown'
	'Spider'
	Gypsophila paniculata
	'Bristol Fairy'

Three-tiered arrangement

FOLIAGE	FLOWERS
cupressus (golden)	2 *Lilium* 'Sterling Star'
Hedera helix 'Silver Queen' (ivy)	2 stems of each of above mentioned varieties of spray chrysanthemum
	3 stems cream spray carnation
	5 white carnation

A closer view of the pulpit shows how the ring of flowers which decorates the font has been echoed. Polythene 'sausages' (mechanics no. 4) are tied to the carving in the wood and hold the ring of daisy chrysanthemums intermingled with cupressus, ivy, white heather and gypsophila. Hanging from a hook on the wall above is a large plaque of flowers (mechanics no. 7).

FOLIAGE	FLOWERS
cupressus (golden)	7 cream spray carnation
Mahonia aquifolium	5 white carnation
Pinus lambertiana (sugar pine)	7 spray chrysanthemum 'Bonnie Jean'
Prunus lusitanica 'Otto Luyken'	7 spray chrysanthemum double white
Prunus lusitanica 'Variegata'	7 *Lilium* 'Sterling Star'

St John's, Woking; nave

A society wedding is about to take place in the chapel of Eton College. A ring of flowers encircled the wrought iron college candelabra, which is one of eight placed at intervals in the choir stalls. Floral foam cut to fit the circle was wrapped in thin polythene and then taped tightly in a number of places so that it was firmly fixed. A delicate arrangement of white flowers and small foliage was topped with lighted candles.

For each candlestand

FOLIAGE	FLOWERS
cupressus	*Alchemilla mollis* (lady's mantle)
Hedera helix 'Silver Queen' (ivy)	*Achillea ptarmica* 'The Pearl'
Hebe anomala (shrubby veronica)	*Gypsophila paniculata* 'Bristol Fairy'
	5 stems white spray carnations (split up)
	7 *Rosa* 'Jack Frost'

Lengths of flat-based, plastic guttering containing floral foam cut in small sections, with a gap between each to allow for easy watering, were placed along the choir stalls. To create the effect of foliage and flowers flowing over the stalls, the height of the floral foam should be at least 5 cm (2 in) above the top of the guttering (mechanics no. 20a and 20b).

In the background one can see part of the beautiful wall paintings which depict miracles of the Virgin. They were the work of at least four master painters who, with their assistants, finally completed them in 1487 after many years of work. In 1560 they were whitewashed over by the college barber acting on the instructions of the new Protestant church authorities, who did not approve of pictures of fictitious miracles. The paintings remained obscured and forgotten for nearly 300 years before being rediscovered and, even then, they were half hidden by the stall canopies. In 1923 these were removed, and the paintings cleaned and restored so that their full beauty and significance could be appreciated.

Choir stalls

FOLIAGE	FLOWERS
Euonymus fortunei radicans 'Silver Queen'	*Achillea ptarmica* 'The Pearl'
Hedera helix 'Silver Queen' (ivy)	*Alchemilla mollis* (lady's mantle)
hosta (plantain lily)	white spray carnations
Weigela florida 'Variegata'	cream spray carnations
	Gypsophila paniculata 'Bristol Fairy'
	Lilium 'Sterling Star'

Eton College Chapel; choir stalls

On either side of the chancel steps we placed a pair of 4.5 m (15 ft) high, L-shaped columns of flowers, one of which is seen here (mechanics no. 24).

FOLIAGE
Dryopteris filix-mas (male fern)
Fagus sylvatica (common beech)
hosta (plantain lily)
Sedum spectabile 'Autumn Joy' (picked before flowering)

FLOWERS
15 white carnation
30 chrysanthemum 'Bonnie Jean'
 7 chrysanthemum 'White Spider'
30 *Lilium* 'Connecticut King'

Eton College Chapel; column of flowers

The service over, the guests descended the impressive oak staircase, on which are carved the names of many hundreds of scholars spanning generations of Etonians. The guests left through a very fine oak doorway dating back to 1482, where we displayed a colourful and be-ribboned wedding circle of flowers (mechanics no. 12).

FOLIAGE
Artemisia arborescens (southernwood)
Buxus sempervirens 'Elegantissima' (box)

FLOWERS
Alchemilla mollis (lady's mantle)
apricot carnations
mixed dwarf bedding dahlias
garden roses

Eton College Chapel; ring of flowers

How to speed up the receiving line at a reception is a recurring problem – most people like to meet the parents of both the bride and groom, and it is the bride's prerogative on this occasion to be told how lovely she looks and the bridegroom how lucky he is. At a recent wedding I attended, the bride's two sisters, who were both bridesmaids and standing in the receiving line, almost reached screaming point when the 200th guest said with a knowing smile: 'And which one of you will be the next bride?'. The idea of serving wine, or even champagne, to the waiting line of guests becomes more and more popular, though often they wait in such chilly winds that a cup of hot soup would be more appreciated!

However, the guests arriving at the beautiful Tudor Suite at Hever Castle in Kent waited in the comfort of the long, carpeted corridors and enjoyed the marvellous pictures and furnishings as they slowly wended their way to the reception area. Here, they passed an all-white arrangement in a white, cherub container set against the dark panelling on a antique side table.

FOLIAGE

Lonicera caprifolium 'Belgica' (honeysuckle)
Eucalyptus gunnii (gum tree)
Sedum spectabile 'Autumn Joy' (picked before flowering)

FLOWERS

3 white agapanthus
5 *Astrantia major* (masterwort)
7 cream carnation
7 chrysanthemum 'Bonnie Jean'
5 green double spray chrysanthemum
3 *Chrysanthemum maximum* (ox-eye daisy)
5 *Lilium* 'Sterling Star'
5 *Molucella laevis* (bells of Ireland)
5 *Nicotiana* 'Sensation' mixed (tobacco plant)
7 *Nicotiana alata* 'Lime Green' (tobacco plant)
5 white *Matthiola* 'Brompton Strain' (stock)

Hever Castle; oak table

Receiving lines

Hever Castle; View of reception room

The scene was set in this beautiful drawing room, where the colouring of the flowers was chosen to complement the furnishings. We placed a pedestal beside the cake table, which stood in the bay window, as we felt that this was the perfect setting for the bride and bridegroom to cut the cake.

Pedestal

FOLIAGE

Dryopteris filix-mas (male fern)
erica (heather)
Eucalyptus gunnii (gum tree)
Lonicera nitida 'Baggesen's Gold'
Sorbaria arborea (false spiraea)

FLOWERS

2 *Antirrhinum majus* 'Madame Butterfly' (snapdragon)
2 gladioli 'Spring Green'
   Nicotiana alata 'Sensation' mixed (tobacco plant)
5 heads hydrangea
10 pink larkspur
2 stems *Crinum × powellii*
7 *Papaver rhoeas* (annual poppy seed heads)
2 phlox
1 *Rosa* 'Pink Peace'
5 *Rosa* 'Peau Douce'
2 *Rosa* 'Queen Elizabeth'
9 florist's rose 'The Bride'
5 garden climber rose 'Handel'
5 *Zinnia elegans*

The wood panelling of the chimney breast provided the ideal background for the pair of plaques which hung at each corner.

For each fireplace plaque

FOLIAGE

Erica arborea alpina (heather)
Hedera helix 'Silver Queen' (ivy)

FLOWERS

5 *Astrantia major* (masterwort)
1 stem pink spray carnation
1 stem florist's buff spray chrysanthemum
5 *Freesia × hybrid* 'Fantasy'
3 *Rosa* 'Bridal Pink'
3 dwarf double zinnia

A plant saucer was fitted into the wrought iron top of each fire-dog, the finished arrangements enhancing the fireplace without taking up valuable space in the room.

Fire-dogs

FOLIAGE
Dryopteris filix-mas (male fern)
Hedera helix 'Silver Queen' (ivy)
Hypericum 'Hidcote' (St John's wort)
Macleaya microcarpa (plume poppy)
Tamarix gallica (tamarisk)
Vinca major (periwinkle)

FLOWERS
Astrantia major (masterwort)
Alstroemeria 'Ligtu Hybrids' (Peruvian lily)
Antirrhinum majus 'Madame Butterfly' (snapdragon)
pale pink spray carnations
florist's pink spray chrysanthemum
geranium flowers
Clarkia amoena 'Sybil Sherwood' (godetia)
Nicotiana alata 'Lime Green' (tobacco plant)
phlox
Rosa 'Bridal Pink'
garden roses
Zinnia elegans dwarf double mixed

The bay window was an ideal position for the wedding cake, which was iced in pale peach and topped with an arrangement of dainty flowers in a small, flat container.

Top of cake table

FOLIAGE
Erica arborea alpina (heather)
Hedera helix 'Marmorata Minor' (ivy)

FLOWERS
white agapanthus, single flowers
larkspur (petite buds and flowers)
Polygonum affine (knotweed)
Rosa 'Cecile Brunner'

Three posies pinned to the cloth were made up of similar plant material bound together and were placed in position on the morning of the wedding.

The tablecloth

The table is 76 cm (30 in) in diameter and stands 73 cm (29 in) from the floor.

A length of sheeting measuring 2.30 m (7 ft 6 in) was cut into a circle, and stitched all the way round 1.2 cm (^{1}/$_2$ in) in from the edge. A tape drawstring was threaded through and pulled up to create a soft hemline before the flounces were made.

Hever Castle; close-up of cake

FOLIAGE
Cotoneaster franchetii
Dryopteris filix-mas (male fern)
Origanum vulgare (marjoram, in flower)

FLOWERS
Alstroemeria 'Ligtu Hybrids' (Peruvian lily)
pink spray carnations
pink carnations
Dahlia 'Preference', 'Love's Dream', 'Swiss Miss'
pink larkspur
garden roses

We could not resist exploring the corridors to discover where the bride would change, and we came across an elegant bedroom with its decor of soft pinks and yellows. Her dress was lying on the chaise longue and beside it we placed a pyramid of flowers, which, reflected in the mirror, instilled an atmosphere of rest and relaxation.

In contrast, the atmosphere of the bridegroom's bathroom inspired us to enjoy a moment of frivolity! This striking, scarlet bath with gold swan taps allowed our imaginations to run riot. We hoped that champagne, red roses and a foam bath would combine to calm the nerves of the bridegroom.

FOLIAGE
Dryopteris filix-mas (male fern)
Hedera colchica 'Dentata' (ivy)
hosta (plantain lily)

FLOWERS
8 *Rosa* 'Jaguar'

Hever Castle; bride's bedroom

Hever Castle; groom's bathroom

Often, the gift of a bouquet of roses is marred when they hang their heads the next day, clearly in need of urgent attention. There is an almost certain cure: cut the stems at an angle and plunge them into 2.5 cm (1 in) of boiling water, holding them for a count of thirty, whilst protecting the blooms from the steam. Transfer them to a deep container which will hold sufficient water to cover the stems and leave them overnight. By morning, they should be restored to their former beauty.

Flowers should enhance the bride, not overshadow her

CHAPTER FOUR

Autumn weddings

UP AND down the country, in towns and villages alike, wedding receptions are held in local halls where, because of their often austere décor, extra thought is required in the planning of the floral decoration. Frequently, one has to contend with a stage and the inevitable velvet curtains, stacks of chairs and series of trestle tables.

In the village hall shown here the rust-coloured curtains were an excellent background for the autumn wedding flowers. Two pairs of hanging stands above and on each side of the buffet table held baskets, each containing one block of floral foam placed horizontally and wrapped in thin polythene. These unusual baskets, their shape resembling hay racks, were filled with autumn foliage and flowers and created a spectacular set piece. A large basket of flowers on the table inside the entrance of the hall greeted the guests as they arrived. Most of the flowers were gathered from local gardens and included chrysanthemums, late summer roses, several varieties of soft peach and apricot dahlias, pale pink hydrangeas, sprays of blackberry (with fruits) and old man's beard.

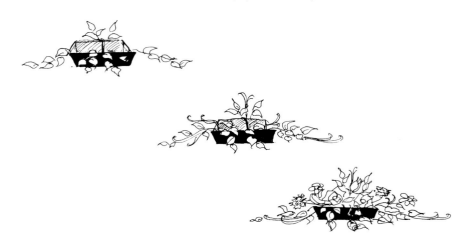

FOLIAGE

Berberis thunbergii 'Atropurpurea Superba'
Clematis vitalba (old man's beard)
Dryopteris filix-mas (male fern)
Hedera canariensis (ivy)
Ligustrum sinense 'Variegatum' (privet)
peony foliage
Symphoricarpos (snowberry)
Weigela florida 'Variegata'

FLOWERS

3 bunches apricot spray carnations
fruiting sprays wild blackberry
garden chrysanthemums
Dahlia 'Preference', 'Pontiac', 'Jean
Fairs', 'Corydon'
small heads of hydrangeas
garden roses

Grayshott Village Hall; buffet table

Close-up of table centre and bridal plaque

An arrangement in a flat basket without a handle, incorporating six orange and peach candles of different lengths, was placed in the centre of the table. The candles were put directly into the floral foam by fixing cocktail sticks round their base with clear adhesive tape (mechanics no. 21).

Hanging in front of the table this unique wedding plaque, meticulously worked in natural plant material, showed the bride and bridegroom's initials and the date of the wedding. It had a dual purpose: not only was it a charming decoration for the buffet table but it also served as a wonderful keepsake of the wedding day. As such, we have featured it in the chapter on Happy Memories (pages 129–134) where we have described how it was made. Similar plaques can decorate marquees or may be hung on the door of a church.

A basket of flowers placed by the entrance door (not pictured) was arranged with garden foliage and flowers in the same autumn colouring and included sheaves of corn, fruit, berries and nuts. When arranging a basket it is important not to cover the handle – it should always look like 'a basket of flowers', able to be picked up by its handle.

And so, we have set the scene for a country wedding. The village hall rent is paid, the bills for the food and drink *will* be paid and, apart from three bunches of spray carnations, all the flowers were gifts from friends and neighbours, with foliage picked from gardens and hedgerows. Here, certainly, maximum effect was achieved with minimum cost.

Another day and another wedding...

Garlands followed the curve of this beautiful staircase down which the bride would walk, and were attached to the banisters in five places on each side. The two plaques hanging at the bottom were fixed over the newel posts with brown string, providing trailing bouquets as finishing touches to the garlands. To give warmth to the white and cream flowers a few pale pink and apricot spray carnations and dahlias were added, and the richer pink of the excellent shrub neillia, which was tucked in at intervals throughout, gave an even greater depth of colour. A close-up of the garland shows the necessity for covering the mechanics carefully, and plenty of short-stemmed foliage and flowers should be used (mechanics no. 4 and 6b).

A charming swan vase on the windowsill at the top of the stairs was arranged with flowers and foliage to match the garlands. The material flowing down over the ledge gave the impression that this swan had a tail.

FOLIAGE
cupressus
Euonymus fortunei radicans 'Silver Queen'
Hebe anomala (shrubby veronica)
Hedera helix 'Glacier' (ivy)
Ligustrum sinense 'Variegatum' (privet)
Neillia longiracemosa

FLOWERS
Aster ericoidus 'Monte Casino'
    (Michaelmas daisy)
chrysanthemum 'Bonnie Jean'
white and pink spray carnations
freesias
Gypsophila paniculata 'Bristol Fairy'
Nicotiana alata 'Lime Green' (tobacco
    plant)

A *curving staircase garlanded with flowers*

Close-up of garland

The large arrangement on the piano was done in a flat container, and this close-up shows the beauty of the Casablanca lilies which made a perfect background for the 'receiving line' once the guests had returned from the church.

FOLIAGE
Hedera colchica 'Dentata' (ivy)
hosta (plantain lily)
Dryopteris filix-mas (male fern)

FLOWERS
white/cream carnations
white *Dahlia* 'Hamari Bride',
　'Biddenham Snowball'
white *Matthiola* 'Brompton Strain'
　(stock)
white larkspur
Lilium 'Casablanca'

Close-up of flowers on piano

The buffet table was placed in a corner of a reception room, and with the soft blue curtains we chose to use pale pink and cream flowers arranged in a two-tiered container in the centre. Two posies of flowers hung over the edge of the table at either end. Two ideas here are worthy of note. Firstly, the table was covered with pink silk material and, over that, a cotton lace bedspread. The small amount of pink which showed through was sufficient to enhance the colour scheme of the flowers and the whole made an unusual table covering. Secondly, the posies were fixed to ribbons which were laid across the table, hung over the back and tied to weights. These balanced the posies and allowed them to hang neatly over the front edge without being attached to the cloth.

Seen here at one side of the buffet table, flowers were arranged on a short, wrought iron stand over the top of which had been tied a cone-shaped piece of floral foam encased in wire netting. Short-stemmed flowers and foliage gave the effect of a pyramid but, ideally, the stand should be placed at a higher vantage point within the room (mechanics no. 17b).

FOLIAGE
Berberis thunbergii 'Atropurpurea Superba'
Hedera helix 'Glacier' (ivy)
Origanum vulgare (marjoram, in
   flower)

FLOWERS
Alstroemeria 'Ligtu Hybrids' (Peruvian lily)
pink spray chrysanthemum
Dahlia 'Newby', 'Pontiac'
Rosa 'Bridal Pink'
Lathyrus odoratus (white sweet pea)
Zinnia elegans (dwarf double mixed)

Hever Castle; buffet table

FOLIAGE
cupressus
Hedera colchica 'Sulphur Heart' (ivy)
hosta (plantain lily)
Ligustrum lucidum 'Excelsum Superbum'
   (Chinese or glossy privet)
Lonicera nitida 'Baggesen's Gold'
   (box honeysuckle)
Lysimachia vulgaris (loosestrife
   foliage)
Rosa 'Mermaid' foliage
Sorbaria arborea (false spiraea)
Symphoricarpos rivularis (snowberry)
Polypodium vulgare (wall fern)

FLOWERS
  5 *Alstroemeria* 'Ligtu Hybrids' (Peruvian
      lily)
  5 chrysanthemum 'Bonnie Jean'
  5 cream spray chrysanthemum
10 double pink garden chrysanthemum
      Chrysanthemum parthenium 'Aureum'
      (feverfew)
  9 collerette dahlias
      Gypsophila paniculata 'Bristol Fairy'

St Alban's Church, Hindhead; pulpit

The church chosen for an autumn wedding had a fine pulpit and here it may be seen ringed with flowers, both above and below the main section. Its unusual base, which is hollow, held a large, flat container in the centre, and foliage and flowers were arranged flowing through the arches. Metal tins, which the church had made to fit the ledges of the pulpit, were used for the rings of flowers. The earliest monogram for Christ, the Chi Rho, an abbreviation of the Greek word for Christ combining the initials X and P, is depicted on the fall.

FOLIAGE

Ballota pseudodictamnus

Clematis vitalba (old man's beard, glycerined)

erica (heather)

Hedera canariensis 'Gloire de Marengo' (ivy)

Hedera helix 'Parsley Crested' (ivy)

Hypericum 'Hidcote' (St John's Wort)

Ligustrum sinense 'Variegatum' (privet)

Lysimachia vulgaris (loosestrife foliage)

Pieris japonica 'Variegata'

Pittosporum tenuifolium 'Warnham Gold'

Polypodium vulgare (wall fern)

Pyrus salicifolia 'Pendula' (weeping pear)

FLOWERS

  5 stems pale pink spray carnation

  1 stem white spray carnation

  5 stems single peach spray chrysanthemum

  2 stems single white spray chrysanthemum

  5 double peach garden chrysanthemum

16 gold carnation

11 dahlias

     Gypsophila paniculata 'Bristol Fairy'

     Nicotiana alata 'Lime Green' (tobacco plant)

  7 garden rose

  5 *Schizostylis coccinea* (Kaffir lily)

St Alban's Church, Hindhead; font

Autumn flowers with long trails of ivy, periwinkle and ferns flowing over the edge decorated this modern font. Curved tin containers which fitted the circular rim of the font were used, with a small, flat container for the central arrangement. The pastoral candle standing behind the font was surrounded by similar flowers and foliage arranged in a container which, although it may sound somewhat bizarre, couldn't be more suitable for use with a large candleholder – a tin mousse ring.

More mousse rings were used for these church candlesticks which were arranged in rich shades of dark red, with pink dahlias backed by the autumnal tinted foliage. Set on the red carpet in this church, they were a wonderful backdrop for the retinue of bridesmaids, who wore deep red, velvet dresses.

FOLIAGE
Berberis thunbergii atropurpurea
Cupressus macrocarpa
Cotoneaster adpressus praecox
Dryopteris filix-mas (male fern)
Fuchsia magellanica gracilis
Lonicera nitida 'Baggesen's Gold'
   (box honeysuckle)
Mahonia bealei

FLOWERS
buff double chrysanthemums
Dahlia 'Doris Day', 'Newby', 'Pontiac'
Nerine bowdenii (Guernsey lily)

St Alban's Church, Hindhead; candlestands

A pensive study of this beautiful Casablanca lily and one little page's contemplation seems all absorbing. Had he plucked it from the arrangement above? Was he thinking that one day *he* might be a flower arranger? I think I can say that this is most improbable, for this is my grandson who, aged three years, was a very well behaved page at a wedding where his father was best man. However, it was not the easiest task to get him into this smart, cream silk sailor suit – he does not like new clothes at the best of times!

CHAPTER FIVE

Winter weddings

OUR CHOICE for a December wedding was the romantic setting of Hever Castle in Kent. The oldest part of the castle was built in 1270, and 200 years later a Tudor dwelling house was added within the original gatehouse and moat, which was crossed by a wooden drawbridge. This was the home of the Bullen family and Anne Boleyn (or Bullen), who may have been born at Hever in 1507, was their second daughter.

It was to become the setting for a love affair which is part of British history and, as one steps over the drawbridge today and into the courtyard, it is very easy to look back through the centuries and to visualize a similar drawbridge over the same moat and all those who have crossed it. One can almost hear the hunting horn blown by King Henry VIII as he rode from the Kent hills, heralding his approach to the castle, for in 1527 he was tiring of his wife Catherine and was pursuing his new love, Anne Boleyn, at Hever. As his horse's hooves clattered over the cobbled yard beneath her bedroom window, so one can imagine her leaning out to greet him.

Henry's marriage to Anne Boleyn was short lived and the 'Bride of a Thousand Days' was beheaded in May 1536. No such fate will befall our twentieth-century Christmas bride and today, in this same courtyard, her guests make their way between a pair of 2.7 m (9 ft) high topiary trees as they walk over the drawbridge.

A topiary tree is really a flower ball on a stick. There should be a base or frame of foliage, some long pieces and some short which will cover the polythene-covered floral foam. In this case variegated holly, sugar pine and cupressus have been used. The sprays of white chrysanthemums are then inserted and the long-tailed ribbon bow is wired and added at the end (mechanics no. 14).

The bride and bridegroom welcome their guests standing by a wedding Christmas tree decorated entirely with silver and white baubles and tinsel. In place of a Christmas fairy, silver wedding bells and bows top the tree and small bunches of fresh gypsophila were inserted into orchid tubes and tucked at intervals amongst the branches. Nowadays, guests often arrive with wedding presents, so they may be placed appropriately under the tree.

Topiary tree

FOLIAGE
cupressus (green and golden)
Ilex aquifolium 'Argentea Marginata'
    (holly)
Pinus lambertiana (sugar pine)

FLOWERS
 9 chrysanthemum 'Bonnie Jean'

Hever Castle; drawbridge

Hever Castle; Christmas tree

In the grand setting of the dining hall at Hever a formal dinner party was laid for the wedding breakfast. The centrepiece was a tall, silver candelabra, into the top of which we fixed a container. This was arranged with white and cream flowers and, to complement the red-edged table mats, a few white and red picot-edged spray carnations were added to the arrangement. Circling the base of the candelabra was a 40 cm (16 in) diameter floral foam ring and this was arranged with similar flowers and foliage. The flowers were put in almost geometrically and heads of cream poinsettias placed at regular intervals were interspersed with white roses, cream carnations and berried holly to give a touch of Christmas. Poinsettia blooms which are picked and used as cut flowers can, if treated properly, have almost as long a life off the plant as on. They are a euphorbia and need to be treated as such, *i.e.* the flower should be picked and held in 2.5 cm (1 in) of boiling water to a count of thirty and then placed in deep water before use. Even after this, if the flower should wilt it may be revived by repeating the treatment.

The arrangements at either end of the table were done in flat silver entrée dishes with flowers and foliage similar to those in the candelabra.

Hever Castle; banqueting table

Candelabra

FOLIAGE
Asparagus densiflorus 'Sprengeri'
cupressus
Hedera helix 'Silver Queen' (ivy)
Ilex aquifolium (holly)
Ilex aquifolium 'Argentea Marginata'
    (variegated holly)

FLOWERS
cream picot-edged spray carnations
cream carnations
Gypsophila paniculata 'Bristol Fairy'
Euphorbia pulcherrima (poinsettia)
Rosa 'Jack Frost'

Mantelpiece

FOLIAGE
Asparagus sprengeri
Danae racemosa (ruscus)
Eucalyptus gunnii (gum tree)
Salix caprea (pussy willow)

FLOWERS
 5 stems apricot spray carnation
 3 cream carnation
 5 stems single peach spray
    chrysanthemum
 7 stems 'White Spider' chrysanthemum
10 Freesia × hybrid
    Gypsophila paniculata 'Bristol Fairy'
10 lemon jonquil narcissus
 2 Lilium 'Stargazer'
 3 pink mini orchid
 3 double white tulip

The beautiful candelabra is shown more clearly in a close-up of the table centre (*see* mechanics no. 12 for the ring at the base).

In an equally elegant setting at Fishmongers Hall in London, a bride adjusted her train as she awaited the arrival of her guests. She stood by this beautiful mantelpiece, on which there were a magnificent clock, gilt candle lights and a large and flowing flower arrangement. The flowers were arranged in a heavy, flat container and their colouring echoed that of the roses used in her headdress.

Christmas is, perhaps, one of the loveliest times to decorate a church and when it is combined with a wedding there is an excuse for something rather special. Invariably, a large pedestal is placed by the altar and for this wedding one was done with a mass of variegated holly, holly with red berries, sugar pine and white flowers (not pictured). As the bride and groom set out on their new life together from the chancel steps, so we emphasized their importance with borders of three-tier stands, one tall and two shorter, which created the impression of a gateway (mechanics no. 25a and 25b). In the photograph just one side of the gateway is shown.

FOLIAGE

Hedera helix 'Silver Queen' (ivy)
Ilex aquifolium 'Argentea Marginata' (holly)
Pinus lambertiana (sugar pine)

FLOWERS

 8 stems white spray carnation
10 white carnation
 8 white spray chrysanthemum
 3 *Euphorbia pulcherrima* (poinsettia)
10 *Rosa* 'Jack Frost'

St Luke's Church, Grayshott; chancel steps

Similar Christmas flowers and foliage have been used in this two-tier stand and a pair of them were placed at facing ends of the choir stalls (mechanics no. 26).

Two-tiered stand

To illustrate the versatility of a floral foam ring, the same one as used round the candelabra at Hever now hangs upright against a lectern (mechanics no. 12).

Nowhere have we described the decoration of church pillars and these *can* present problems. Ideas vary to how they should be adorned with flowers: florettes attached by fishing line to the capitals can be hung down the pillars, garlands can be used to form spirals around them and parcels of moss can encircle the capitals.

This purpose-built container, made to fit the capital of the pillar, is one of the most satisfactory mechanics we have found for such decoration. Here, it is shown as used for the Christmas wedding, with wet floral foam, and if sufficient space is left for easy watering, the circle of foliage and flowers will keep fresh for many days.

The method is as follows: firstly, place long, flowing branches of variegated holly and trails of ivy so that they hang down and away from the pillar. Fill in the centre with different lengths of cupressus and sugar pine, ensuring that they point in different directions. Flowers of varying lengths should then be added so that the general effect is loose and informal (mechanics no. 15a and 15b).

St Luke's Church, Grayshott; pillar encircled with flowers

FOLIAGE
Asparagus plumosus (asparagus fern)
cupressus
Hedera helix 'Silver Queen' (ivy)
Ilex aquifolium 'Argentea Marginata' (holly)
Pinus lambertiana (sugar pine)

FLOWERS
12 cream carnation
14 pink carnation
12 chrysanthemum 'Bonnie Jean'
 6 Euphorbia pulcherrima (poinsettia)
12 Rosa 'Jack Frost'
 Gypsophila paniculata 'Bristol Fairy'

These types of mechanics can be used easily at any time of the year. In spring, catkins and palm may be hung from the container as well as sprays of forsythia and blossom. Soft-stemmed spring flowers such as daffodil, narcissus and tulip can be inserted into floral foam more easily if a hole is made first with a skewer or hard stick. For summer weddings, unlimited varieties of flower and foliage may be used to suit the colour scheme but, equally, the arrangement can look attractive with just 'Bonnie Jean' spray chrysanthemums, cow parsley and gypsophila. Again, there is endless scope for autumn weddings – trails of ivy, blackberry, old man's beard, rose hips and berries, all interspersed with the beautiful autumnal colours found in garden dahlias, chrysanthemums, drying hydrangeas and late summer roses.

With regard to old man's beard – what a delightful plant to find in our hedgerows – remember to pick it at the right moment, that is, while still green and before becoming fluffy. It can be used to great effect if you remove all the leaves, as they detract from the daintiness of the florets. Use this way or preserve for use throughout the winter as follows. First cut the stems at an angle and place them in a container with one part glycerine to two parts hot water, making sure that the mixture has been

Grayshott; ring on lectern

stirred thoroughly to prevent separation. Leave in a dry place for up to two weeks, by which time the stems will be brown and the florets perfectly preserved and flexible. A tip for the festive season – hold the glycerined old man's beard over newspaper and spray with white paint. Quickly, while still wet, shake silver glitter over it and this will give a charming, sparkly effect which will look delightful in Christmas arrangements.

A variety of mature, undamaged plant material can also be preserved by this method and, being cream and brown rather than fresh green, it can create an unusual colour scheme. Probably the most successful months for glycerining are July and August, when the sap is still rising. Listed below are some of the most popular varieties for glycerining:

FOLIAGE
aspidistra (stand in glycerine for 6-8
   weeks, spongeing leaves
   occasionally with the mixture)
bergenia (sponge leaves occasionally)
broom
buxus (box)
castanea (sweet chestnut)
Choisya ternata (Mexican orange
   blossom)
cotoneaster
cupressus
elaeagnus
eucalyptus (gum tree)
Fagus sylvatica (beech)
fatshedera
Fatsia japonica (sponge leaves
   occasionally)
grevillea
hedera (sponge leaves occasionally)
hellebore
Laurus nobilis (laurel)
mahonia
montbretia
Pittosporum tenuifolium
quercus (oak)

SEED HEADS AND FLOWERS
Alchemilla mollis (lady's mantle)
aquilegia
delphinium
honesty (picked when green)
hydrangea (picked when crisp in autumn)
lime flowers
Molucella laevis (bells of Ireland) (stand in
   glycerine for 2-3 days, then hang
   upside down)
montbretia
pampas
papaver (annual poppy)
verbascum

Bleached and commercially dried foliage and seed heads are easily obtainable. To ensure that the stems do not rot when using with fresh plant material, dip the ends in melted candle wax and, when not in use, store them in *dry* conditions to prevent mildew.

As we come to the end of the year, you can see how everything shown in this book may be adapted easily for each season, for all settings, for all types of wedding and for all sizes of pocket. I hope we have illustrated how the beauty of a lily or the simplicity of a garden dahlia can be used to create flowers for weddings with equal success.

CHAPTER SIX

Mechanics

I HAVE already mentioned belts and braces in referring to the mechanics used for flower arranging. I regard these as quite the most important part of the whole operation, for, whatever the circumstances, the plant material must remain rigidly in place and have access to good water-retaining material to ensure that it remains fresh. This is only possible if the utmost care is given to the design and choice of containers used for the flowers. The pages of drawings show the mechanics for all the arrangements pictured in this book. The descriptions of their construction and uses are numbered and gathered here for easy reference.

1. Long plaque
(a) side view
(b) front view

A piece of wood 1.8 m × 5 cm (6 ft × 2 in) with floral foam cut into strips to fit its length and breadth, is covered with thin polythene and then encased in 5 cm (2 in) gauge wire netting, firmly hooked together all the way down. If used in a church, a strip of narrow foam or bubble plastic is attached to the back to protect the church fabric. Ties of garden string, plastic-covered wire or fishing line along the sides and each end secure the plaque in position. This type of mechanic may be modified in length and breadth to suit a variety of positions.

2. Shorter plaque
(a) front view
(b) side view

This is made as above, but is shorter in length.

3. Garland
This very versatile, curved garland of flowers may be achieved by using

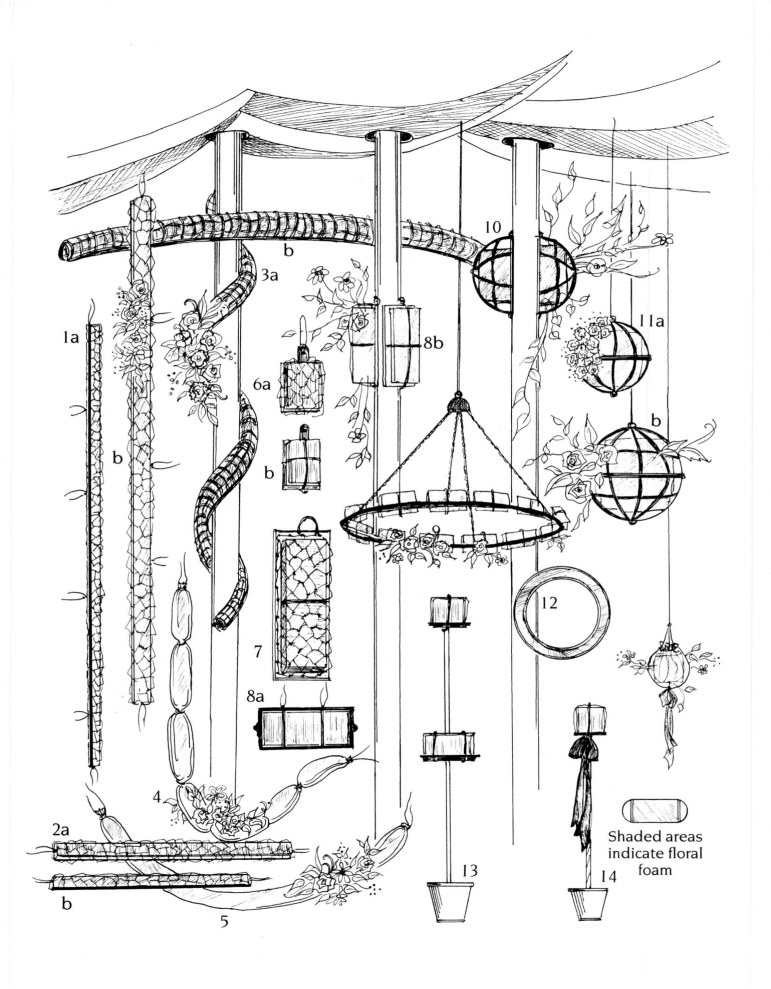

1a

b

2a

b

3a

b

4

5

6a

b

7

8a

8b

9

10

11a

b

12

13

14

Shaded areas
indicate floral
foam

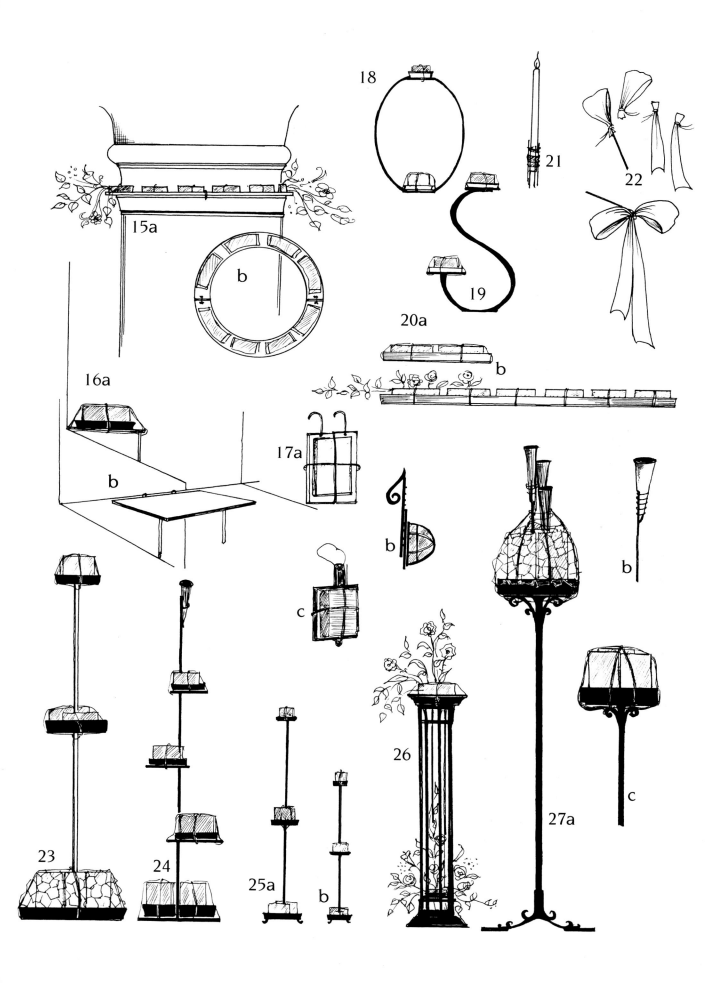

15a

b

16a

b

17a

b

c

18

19

20a

b

21

22

23

24

25a

b

26

27a

b

c

plastic netting joined together with wire to form a tube approximately 10 cm (4 in) in diameter. This is then filled with pieces of floral foam wrapped in thin polythene, interspersed with moss. If the foam is kept damp the spiral can be used several times before replacing with new foam.

(a) Here the garland is shown curling round a marquee pole. It is attached with wire or, more easily, butchers' hooks (available at most kitchen shops), to four evenly-spaced cup hooks screwed into the pole.

(b) This shows the garland curving gently over the entrance to a church or marquee, where it would be attached to the marquee construction or the church porch if there were available fixing points.

4. Garland

Polythene 'sausages' are one of the simplest ways of making smaller, lighter garlands which are often used on choir stalls or along mantelpieces and staircases. Wet floral foam is covered in a continuous length of thin polythene and tied with string or taped at regular intervals to resemble a string of sausages. Sections of foam of equal size may also be put into a series of plastic bags, which are then tied together.

5. Garland

Lengths of polythene tubing of varying dimensions are also available commercially and can be used to create a similar effect to 4.

6. Plaque

(a) A florette case with a block of well-soaked floral foam 10 × 7.5 cm (4 × 3 in) is covered with clingfilm and 5 cm (2 in) gauge wire netting fixed firmly around it. Three such plaques can be attached to nails high up on a marquee pole, providing the basis for a continuous circle of flowers.

(b) As above but without the wire netting; the foam is covered only with polythene and secured with tape. This variation is useful for smaller, lighter plaques.

Florettes are also available complete with foam and cage in two sizes (no diagram).

7. Plaque

This is a length of wood 46 × 20 cm (18 × 8 in), backed with foam or bubble plastic, containing two blocks of foam covered with thin polythene and 5 cm (2 in) gauge wire netting. The netting is bent round nails on the edges of the wood for secure fixing.

8. Plaque

(a) A block of floral foam covered with thin polythene is secured with tape in a special foam tray and ties are added for hanging.

(b) This illustrates three such plaques fixed around a marquee pole.

9. Flower circle

This is a flat, wrought iron circle 84 cm (33 in) in diameter which hangs on chains. Sections of floral foam are covered with thin polythene, fixed alternately to the top and bottom sides of the circle and secured firmly with tape.

10. Flower basket

A third method of decorating a marquee pole is by using two plastic-covered flower baskets, size as required, and both containing foam covered in thin polythene, first fixed either side of the pole and then wired together for extra stability.

11. Flower ball

(a) This is made from a pair of small flower baskets wired together which contain floral foam covered with thin polythene. The ball is shown with a compact arrangement of short-stemmed flowers placed in the foam and a froth of gypsophila surrounding them.

(b) A pair of large, hanging flower baskets (plastic-covered) enclosing a jumbo block of floral foam, well soaked and wrapped in thin polythene, are wired together very firmly. If jumbo foam is not obtainable, four standard-sized blocks would be equivalent. When the ball is finished, full of flowers and foliage, it could weigh up to 16.3 kg (36 lbs) and be at least 91 cm (3 ft) in diameter. Careful hanging is necessary and a shackle in the top of the ball with a double nylon rope is advised.

(c) A piece of foam 10 × 7.6 cm (4 × 3 in) is wrapped in thin polythene and moss tucked into the bottom and sides. The whole is then enclosed in 4 × 2.5 cm (1½ × 2 in) gauge wire netting and long stub wires, attached to four points, are twisted together to ensure that it hangs evenly.

12. Florist's circle

A florist's circle is available in four different sizes and comprises a plastic base with a continuous line of floral foam. If covered with thin polythene before use, the life of the plant material will be prolonged.

13. Two-tiered tree

This is made in detachable sections for easy transportation. A metal rod is set in concrete or similar fixative in a bucket or large, plastic flower pot so that 7.5 cm (3 in) extends above the finished surface. Then, short lengths of hollow metal tubing are soldered to the centres of two shallow tins, one on the underside and the other on both sides. These slot into two 60 cm (2 ft) lengths of slightly larger metal rod which, in turn, fit into the base. The stems are wrapped in toning shades of florist's ribbon, and white granite chips (available in small

quantities at large garden centres) are put in the top of the flower pot to hide the cement.

14. Topiary tree

A wooden pole, length and diameter dependent upon the required size, is inserted into a flower pot or large tin filled with cement or cellulose filler. A layer of stones at the base provides extra weight and stability, particularly for larger trees. A small platform is fixed to the top of the pole to take a piece of floral foam wrapped in thin polythene. Before arranging, the pole is painted a suitable colour. Ribbon can be wound diagonally around the stem and matching bows and tails placed into the tree once the arrangement is complete.

15. Church pillar

(a) This is an excellent construction and can be custom built to fit the capital of any pillar. A circle of wood is cut in two, the halves being joined together with bolts and wing nuts when in position around the pillar. The circle is edged with wood and divided into sections to contain a series of shallow trays. Each tray contains floral foam, well soaked and covered with thin polythene, and the edging is painted to match the pillar. These mechanics provide the perfect basis for a ring of flowers.

(b) This shows the half circles joined together.

16. Platform for a sloping church windowsill

    (a) side view
    (b) front view

This platform with two legs is hooked on to a strip of wood which has been screwed along the top of the sill. A container with a block of foam is taped to the shelf for added safety.

17. Pew ends

(a) A block of floral foam is fixed to a piece of wood and the whole enclosed in a polythene bag and firmly taped. Two hooks, made from stub wires bound together with tape or ribbon to prevent scratching, are shaped to fit over the end of the pew or wherever they are required.

(b) This commercial container is also available. Its length is adjustable and new floral foam may be inserted for re-use. It can also be used over the top of a door, or the handle removed and ribbon threaded through the loop provided for hanging anywhere else.

(c) A florette case containing a block of well-soaked floral foam 10 × 7.5 cm (4 × 3 in) is covered with thin polythene and secured with tape. Ribbon is threaded through the handle for easy hanging.

18. Metal circle

This is a commercially produced container consisting of two metal platforms joined by a metal hoop (available in two sizes).

19. S-shaped stand

This is a purpose-made metal stand with two platforms to take containers.

20. Plastic guttering

(a) and (b) Flat-based, plastic guttering with clip-on ends is readily available from builders' merchants in varying lengths. This is easily cut to the required length and floral foam blocks can be spaced at intervals to allow for easy watering.

21. Candle

Depending on the size of the candle, four barbecue or three cocktail sticks are taped securely to its base to form the supports which can then be put into the floral foam.

22. Bows and tails

Rather than tie a bow with a continuous length of ribbon, it is easier to wire each loop and tail individually and then attach them to a separate stub wire which can be inserted into the floral foam.

23. Large three-tiered stand

Again, this is a specially made stand comprising a solid metal pole 1.5 m (5 ft) high, which is inserted through a shallow container 23 cm (9 in) in diameter and fixed to a circular container 30.5 cm (12 in) in diameter at the base. A platform holds the container for the top arrangement and the three finished arrangements, graded in size, give a three-tiered effect, rather like a wedding cake.

24. Column

The column consists of a metal stand, base, platforms (the number of which depends on the finished height required), and a circle at the top to hold a cone. This is the ideal basis for a column of flowers, the back shelves providing balance and depth.

25. Three-tiered container

(a) This shop-bought stand is ideal for buffet tables, etc.

(b) A similar stand is also available in a smaller size.

26. Metal torchère

This unusual, commercially produced container is made of slender, wrought iron bars and permits two placements. It holds a large container on the top and a saucer of floral foam inside the base, which allows the flowers to flow up through the centre and out through the bars.

27. Pedestal

(a) The mechanics for a large pedestal are very personal to the arranger but, first and foremost, they must be strong enough to hold a large

amount of plant material. I like to wedge two or three blocks of floral foam into the pedestal top, leaving adequate space at the sides of the container for easy watering. Wire netting, 4–5 cm (1½–2 in) gauge, then covers the whole container and is tied firmly underneath. Three cones are inserted at different levels towards the back of the foam and all are taped together.

(b) This sketch depicts a cone taped to a stick to give extra height.

(c) For a medium-sized arrangement, wedge blocks of floral foam into the pedestal top (allowing sufficient space for watering) and tape them firmly in place.

The sketches of mechanics mentioned in the Royal Wedding chapter refer to those diagrams that I did at the time for the benefit of the Clerk of Works and the arrangers who would be using them. They are not numbered as the diagrams of mechanics described in this chapter, but it may be of interest to recognize some of the more notable structures used in Westminster Abbey, such as the organ loft archway, the metal triangles for the organ loft, the choir stalls, and the arrangements above and beyond the high altar.

CHAPTER SEVEN

Beginners only

THIS CHAPTER is not meant for the experienced flower arranger, who may have looked through the book, referred to the mechanics used and known at once how the arrangement was done. It is a chapter geared towards potential flower arrangers who, admiring some of the designs, would love to do them for their daughters' or friends' weddings but have no idea how to begin. I shall, therefore, describe in detail how I would do certain flower arrangements, not dictating how they *must* be done, but giving guidelines that I hope will prove helpful without restricting personal creativity.

Step-by-step

An arrangement of flowers comprises *five* stages:
1.	Container
2.	Mechanics
3.	Water
4.	Foliage
5.	Flowers

These five stages should be used for any type of arrangement, be it a large pedestal, a small urn or a long, low, flat container and, indeed, these basic guidelines can equally be applied to a plaque, a flower ball, a candleholder or a wreath. So, here are the stages described in turn:

1. Container

The choice depends on the size of arrangement and the position it will occupy. It must be large enough to hold the required amount of plant material, deep enough to take an adequate supply of water, and sturdy enough to remain balanced when full. A container that is visible must be in proportion with the height of the arrangement and must harmonize with the finished design. An unseen container can range from a loaf tin or steak and kidney dish (painted a neutral shade), to a

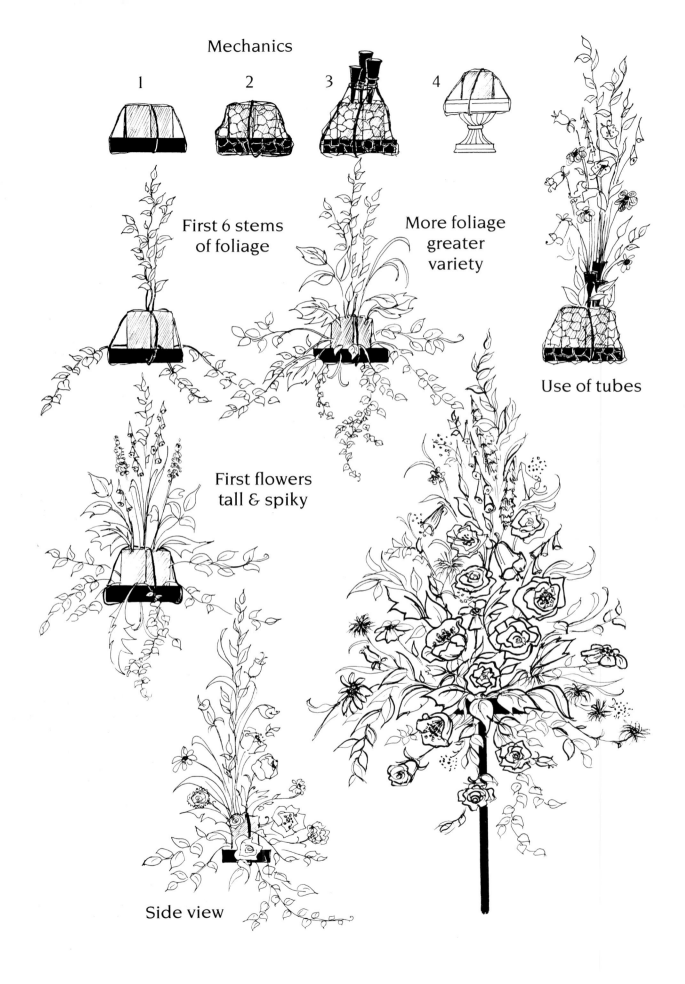

Mechanics

1   2   3   4

First 6 stems
of foliage

More foliage
greater
variety

Use of tubes

First flowers
tall & spiky

Side view

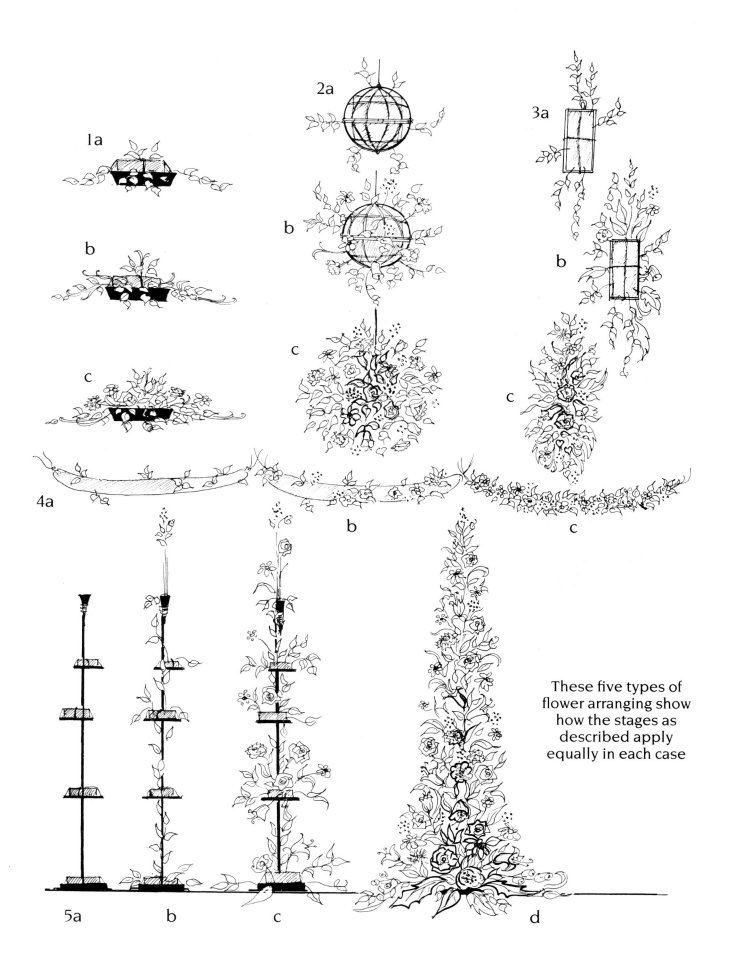

1a

b

c

2a

b

c

3a

b

c

4a

b

c

5a

b

c

d

These five types of flower arranging show how the stages as described apply equally in each case

variety of plastic bowls and, for an even larger arrangement, a washing-up bowl.

2. Mechanics

I have already stressed the importance of these in Chapter Six and I stress it again, for the flowers will topple, whatever the size of the arrangement, if the mechanics are unstable. A well-anchored piece of floral foam in its container is, therefore, essential. It should be cut to fit snugly back and front, leaving space at the sides for the water, and secured with floral-foam tape, string or wire. If heavy plant material is used, stretch a piece of 4 − 5 cm (1½ − 2 in) gauge wire netting, selvedge removed, over the top of the foam and fix it securely as before. Again, if heavy plant material is used and there is also a need to raise shorter stemmed flowers higher in the arrangement, insert one or more tubes attached to canes of the required length in the foam. These should be placed towards the back of the blocks, through the wire netting, and be well taped, if necessary, around the base of the container or the top of the pedestal. Should watering prove difficult owing to the position of the flowers. (*e.g.* pew ends and plaques), then the foam should be pre-soaked and wrapped in thin polythene.

3. Water

Never cram a container with floral foam so that it cannot be watered or topped up easily. Floral foam must never dry out, so fill the containers with water before beginning the arrangement and, if tubes are used, be sure to fill them too as soon as they are fixed − it is easy to forget once the flowers are in position. If someone else is likely to water the arrangement, leave instructions as to how many tubes you have used and where they are. Do *not* overfill the container − nothing is more irritating than a dripping pedestal on a church floor, and this can be made worse if a leaf or stem happens to have been placed on the rim of the container, when quite extensive syphoning may occur.

Remember the advantages of freshening all finished arrangements with a fine mist spray.

4. Foliage

Every flower arrangement should have a frame or outline of foliage to provide the basic shape for a design. Select a variety of textures, shapes, colours and sizes of foliage and divide it into groups. Begin your framework with six main branches, A tall, straight one should be placed upright first, followed by two of differing heights on either side and two curving stems to the left and right. The sixth should be shorter and curving and be placed in the front of the floral foam, flowing forward.

Three or four similar branches of varying lengths should then be placed at the back and sides of the container, since the view of the flower arrangement must be equally good from all angles. Choosing a different type of foliage next, insert five to seven pieces following the

line of the initial branches, but in all cases cutting the stems slightly shorter. Two or three pieces of trailing foliage, such as ivy, may then be inserted to spill over the edge, as this always adds movement to an arrangement. To ensure that the front view is not too flat, place three or four shorter pieces of foliage at different heights and angles. Larger, solid leaves such as bergenia, hosta and fatsia can be added now to give emphasis and substance to the centre of the design.

5. Flowers

Tall, spike-shaped flowers (*e.g.* gladioli, delphiniums, stocks and larkspur) are added first, beginning at the centre-back of the arrangement. Look for curving stems which can be placed well out to the sides, whilst smaller flowers (*e.g.* alstroemeria, spray carnations, spray chrysanthemums) can then fill in the picture within the frame at different heights, lengths and angles. Larger flowers, such as roses, chrysanthemum blooms and dahlias, can form the focal points. Place these last, allowing them to flow through the arrangement, again at varying angles and with different lengths of stem.

These guidelines can easily be adapted to other types of arrangement whether smaller or larger and, in all cases, it will be seen from the diagrams how the framework of foliage in firm mechanics is the basis for the flowers which are added afterwards.

Now for a few words of caution:

- Avoid placing flowers in a position where they look unhappy. The gladiolus, for example, a tall, straight and dignified flower, looks so good if placed in an arrangement upright and at different heights, but most unattractive if inserted at the three points of a triangle, the two lower corners facing downwards. Once gladioli are put in this position nothing will soften the angular line of the arrangement.

- Avoid also the 'bulbous' arrangement, sometimes likened to a pregnant mum. This happens when all the flowers are placed facing outwards at similar levels. A few shorter stemmed flowers recessed and other blooms turned slightly sideways will make a dramatic difference.

- Do not feel obliged to get your full money's worth out of every stem of spray chrysanthemums by using them as they are. Often there are too many flowers and buds at the same level, so by carefully removing one or two of these and equally carefully putting them on one side, the main stem will look less heavy in the arrangement and the little flowers will be ideal for table decorations.

Tips

General

1. Where possible arrange flowers *in situ*, taking care that the design looks good from all angles. It is helpful to walk away from your arrangement for a few minutes as often, on returning with a fresh eye, one can see obvious mistakes.

2. Gather flowers and foliage from the garden in the early morning or evening, avoiding the midday sun, and put them straight into a bucket of water. Stand the bucket in a cool place overnight.

3. Always cut stems at an angle of 45° as this provides a point with which to pierce the floral foam and, gives a larger area of cut stem through which the flower can drink. Carnations must be cut between nodules.

4. All lower leaves should be removed from the stems of flowers and foliage before conditioning as they decay under water and cause stagnation. Also the stripped end of a stem is always easier to insert into the mechanics.

5. Flowers take up the greatest amount of water during the first few hours after arranging. It is important, therefore, to top up within 24 hours of having completed the arrangement.

Conditioning garden material

1. Foliage will last very much longer if time is spent carefully conditioning. Always slit, crush or hammer the ends of woody stems before plunging them into water for an overnight drink. This process allows the water to penetrate the stem fibre.

2. Immature foliage needs more drastic conditioning to prevent it wilting. Place the ends of the stems in 2.5 cm (1 in) of boiling water for 30 seconds, protecting the foliage from the heat, and then transfer to a bucket of water.

3. Foliage such as euphorbia and cardoon will benefit from singeing or burning the ends of the stems with a candle flame or match until blackened. Poppies will also hold if given this treatment.

4. Hosta leaves and ferns benefit from being submerged in a large container or a bath, if the family has no objection. A teaspoonful of starch added to the water will help to keep the leaves turgid. However, grey foliage is the exception to this method as it will lose its lustre.

5. To condition hollow-stemmed material such as delphiniums, lupins and hollyhocks, fill the upturned stem with water, plug with cotton wool and, keeping the plug in position with your finger, place stems in a bucket of water.

6. To keep tulip stems rigid, wrap them in newspaper up to their necks and place in deep water. Piercing the stem with a pin 2.5 cm (1 in) below the flowerhead may help to keep it erect.

7. Syringa, philadelphus and lilac are less likely to wilt if the leaves are removed, the woody stem crushed at the end and a teaspoonful of lemonade added to the water.

8. To retard flowers such as gladioli, iris, lilies and peonies, lay them on a stone or concrete floor in a darkened area.

9. To advance plant material, particularly longiflorum lilies, place the stems in tepid water and leave in a warm temperature. Ornamental currant, forsythia and spring blossom can be forced if cut when in bud and brought indoors to similar conditions.

10. The heads of hydrangeas and hellebores should be immersed upside-down in water and left for up to five hours. When picking hydrangea bracts, ensure that you cut a section of the woody stem *with* the new growth.

Conditioning florist flowers

1. Roses need great care. First of all, remove the thorns, which makes the stems easier to handle, and follow with the boiling method. Again, as with immature foliage, place the cut and split ends in 2.5 cm (1 in) of boiling water for 30 seconds, making sure that the blooms are carefully covered with tissue paper and kept well away from the heat, and then put in water overnight. Roses can also be revived by this method, as described on page 64.

2. Gerberas are not always reliable unless given special treatment. Boil the stalk ends as before and suspend over a full bucket of water so that the stems are submerged to just below the flowerhead.

3. Removing stamens from lily flowers will prevent the petals or, indeed, one's own clothes, being stained with pollen.

4. To encourage the florets of gladioli to open, remove one or two of the top buds.

DESIGN FOR FLOWERS WESTMINSTER ABBEY
JULY 23rd 1986 FOR THE WEDDING OF
H.R.H PRINCE ANDREW AND MISS SARAH FERGUSON.

1.

THE WEST DOOR

NAVE WINDOW SILLS

St. GEORGE'S CHAPEL

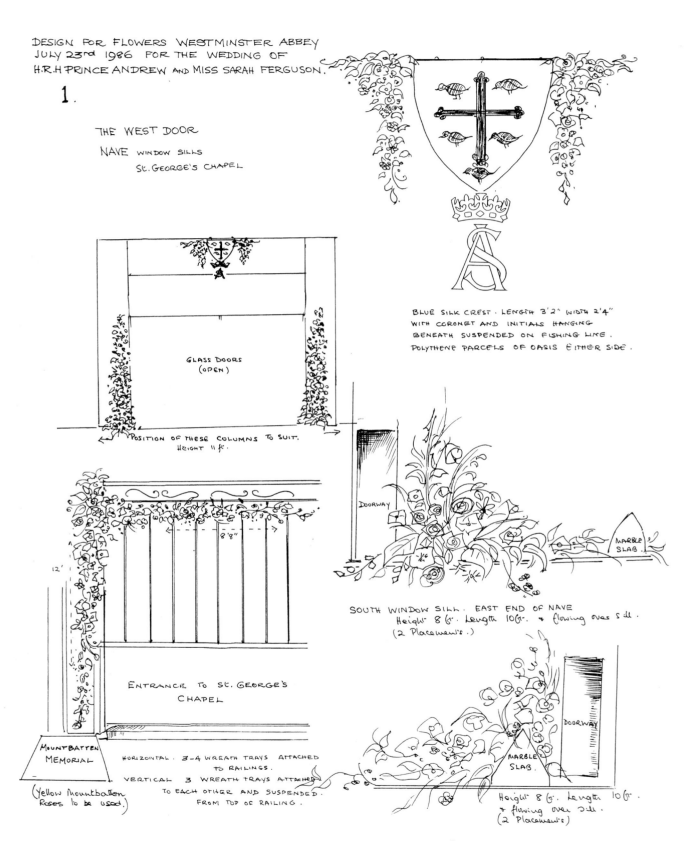

BLUE SILK CREST. LENGTH 3'2" WIDTH 2'4"
WITH CORONET AND INITIALS HANGING
BENEATH SUSPENDED ON FISHING LINE.
POLYTHENE PARCELS OF OASIS EITHER SIDE.

GLASS DOORS
(OPEN)

POSITION OF THESE COLUMNS TO SUIT.
HEIGHT 11 ft.

DOORWAY

MARBLE
SLAB.

SOUTH WINDOW SILL. EAST END OF NAVE
Height 8 ft. Length 10 ft. + flowing over sill.
(2 Placements.)

12'

8'8"

ENTRANCE TO St. GEORGE'S
CHAPEL

MOUNTBATTEN
MEMORIAL

(Yellow Mountbatten
Roses to be used.)

HORIZONTAL. 3-4 WREATH TRAYS ATTACHED
TO RAILINGS.
VERTICAL 3 WREATH TRAYS ATTACHED
TO EACH OTHER AND SUSPENDED
FROM TOP OF RAILING.

DOORWAY

MARBLE
SLAB.

Height 8 ft. Length 10 ft.
+ flowing over sill.
(2 Placements)

NORTH WINDOW SILL. EAST END OF NAVE.

CHAPTER EIGHT

Flowers for a Royal Wedding

MANY DIFFERENT types of wedding have been described, all fairy-tale settings for fairy-tale days, but now I am going to recount a stage set for a wedding with a congregation reaching far beyond these shores. It was a romance which caught the imagination of this country, and echoed around the world, yielding colour and glamour and a sparkling happiness which gladdened the hearts of many thousands of people. They watched, waited and enjoyed every second of the pomp, the pageantry, the glory of the setting, the beauty of the flowers and the charm and happiness of the principal participants.

The wedding of HRH Prince Andrew and Miss Sarah Ferguson took place on 23 July 1986 in Westminster Abbey. The National Association of Flower Arrangement Societies of Great Britain has been responsible for the flowers in the Abbey for all special occasions since 1967. It was not surprising, therefore, that the Receiver General approached me in April 1986, as the then Chairman of NAFAS, to organize the flowers for the wedding.

A week later I met the Prince and his fiancée in the Abbey to discuss their requirements. It was very obvious from the start that they had a great love for flowers and were anxious that these should play an important part in the ceremony. It was necessary that many should be visible from the high camera vantage points which would relay the service around the world. The Prince suggested 'flowers hanging from the roof' and the flower balls which were suspended from the arches in the nave evolved from this idea. Miss Ferguson talked of 'banks of flowers' and she wrote down the colours she wanted to complement her dress as well as her bridesmaids' and pages' outfits and, handing me a piece of paper, she said she hoped they would remain a secret, even from the Prince. I put most of the questions listed in Chapter One (page 16) to the Prince, Miss Ferguson and the Abbey staff, except the slightly inappropriate one of expense, but it became apparent in the subsequent weeks that the sum offered by the

Privy Purse would be more than supplemented by the wonderful gifts of flowers from growers throughout this country, the Channel Islands and overseas.

From this initial meeting I had a fairly definite idea of what was required, though I was somewhat daunted by the enormity of the task. The preparation in the weeks that followed was like a giant jigsaw with the 'pieces' gradually falling into place. The team of flower arrangers was chosen by ballot – the names being taken from each section of the NAFAS organization – and the final list of 45 people from all corners of Great Britain was truly representative of the association as a whole.

By mid-June I had completed the drawings of the designs and delivered them to Buckingham Palace. They were approved enthusiastically, and from then on the limited time available before the day was filled to capacity with lists of lists of things to do! Numbers of flowers were estimated, ordered . . . and then added to. How many buckets would we need? How many blocks of floral foam? Where would we get the foliage? Most important, though, was the need to co-ordinate every single siting of flowers with the exact requirements of the service, the ceremonial and the guests. Large pedestals should not obscure the view of family friends and foreign diplomats and no flowing arrangements should narrow an entrance through which the bridal party would walk. The organist had to be able to see his choir and soloists, the Royal Marine trumpeters herald the bride unimpeded and the line of church dignitaries should not be hampered by over-large arrangements as they received the guests.

In Chapter x the belts and braces of mechanics are described. Here, the mechanics needed to be wider, stronger and, above all, faultless. This was not an occasion for errors as there would be no time to put them right, so it was very important that the detailed instructions given to the flower arrangers were strictly adhered to. The Clerk of Works of the Abbey, understandably, was a formidable task-master, but eventually he acknowledged our attention to detail and agreed to our plans. I think it is not unreasonable to suggest that some of the arrangements were more ambitious and, certainly, more meticulously planned than anything hitherto attempted in the Abbey. It was unusual to plan flowers for a building as large as Westminster Abbey in one colour scheme throughout, yet the lovely white, cream, pale pink, soft peach and apricot chosen by the bride were a perfect foil for the ornate decorations of the Abbey.

The flower balls already mentioned were a great success. There were fourteen in all, each one hanging in the centre of every arch along the length of the nave. To ensure their practical application we had a full dress rehearsal in the Abbey with the Clerk of Works a month prior to the wedding. It was to be the Abbey staff's responsibility to hang the balls on double nylon cord from the triforium and our responsibility to provide suitable rings, shackles and special washers so that there was no risk of them falling to the ground. The basis of each ball was a pair of 35.5 cm (14 in) flower baskets wired together, containing a well-soaked jumbo block of floral foam wrapped in polythene. When complete each weighed a total of 16.3 kg (36 lbs) (see pages 111 and 123).

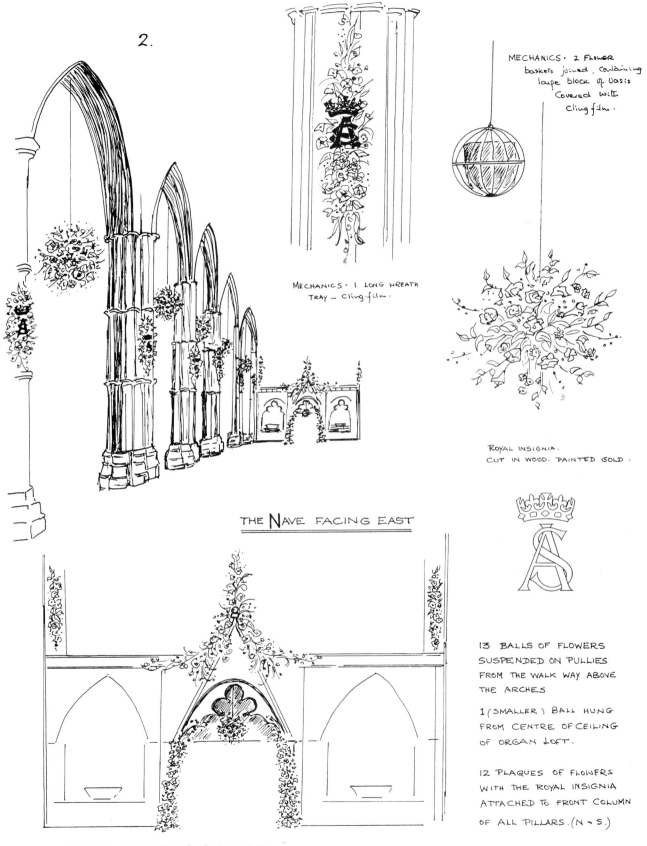

2.

MECHANICS· 2 FLOWER
baskets joined, containing
large block of Oasis
covered with
cling film.

MECHANICS· 1 LONG WREATH
TRAY — cling film.

ROYAL INSIGNIA.
CUT IN WOOD. PAINTED GOLD.

THE NAVE FACING EAST

13 BALLS OF FLOWERS
SUSPENDED ON PULLIES
FROM THE WALK WAY ABOVE
THE ARCHES

1 (SMALLER) BALL HUNG
FROM CENTRE OF CEILING
OF ORGAN LOFT.

12 PLAQUES OF FLOWERS
WITH THE ROYAL INSIGNIA
ATTACHED TO FRONT COLUMN
OF ALL PILLARS. (N & S.)

ARCHWAY AT ENTRANCE OF ORGAN LOFT
SPECIAL STAND · CURVING TO FRAME ENTRANCE.

TOP OF ORGAN LOFT. (SPECIAL FITTING.)
MUST NOT OBSTRUCT TRUMPETERS & CHOIR.

By the morning of Monday 21 July all 14 balls had been suspended 1 – 1.5 m (4 – 5 ft) from the ground with buckets of the allocated flowers underneath in readiness for the arrangers. The first priority was to cover every part of the floral foam, since the polythene could have easily caught the camera and television lights. Next short stems of foliage, alchemilla and spray carnations were inserted. Then, working outwards, longer stems were inserted until, finally, the full-length stems of carnations, spray chrysanthemums, lilies, etc. were added, finishing with gypsophila. The result was magical and I felt that they fitted Prince Andrew's original request perfectly. It spoke well of the jumbo blocks of floral foam that, without watering or spraying between Tuesday and Sunday, many of the flowers remained fresh.

The plaques which hung on the nave pillars were backed with plywood and each took three standard blocks of floral foam, individually wrapped in polythene, with a space between each allowing metal rods to protrude to take the royal cypher. The whole was covered with galvanized wire mesh, and metal clips with cords attached them to the pillars. The cyphers, *i.e.* the crown with intertwined 'A' and 'S', were cut in plywood, painted in two shades of gold and joined by two strips of wood painted green so that they would not be seen amidst the foliage.

Triumphant, high above the nave in the organ loft, were two vast triangular arrangements, one facing west and the other facing east. The initial suggestions for these arrangements were received with anxiety by the Abbey staff (who feared that valuable space would be encroached upon), enthusiastically by the bride and groom, and with determination by myself. It was agreed that if we could evolve suitable mechanics they would be approved.

Behind the huge, ornate gilded apex which faced west was a concrete triangle 10 cm (4 in) deep. A triangular metal frame was made to fit this exactly, on which platforms held containers and a tall rod topped with a ring held a cone (pages 111 and 123). The only screw used in the whole of the Abbey was one put through the base of this triangle into the stone. The accuracy of its fit allowed for the huge, yet graceful arrangement which dominated the nave and was the perfect foil for the Royal Marines who heralded the bride with a fanfare of trumpets.

The east end of the organ loft was quite different. Firstly, the mechanics had to be worked around the organ and there was not triangle of stone on which to fix anything. Two separate constructions resulted: a stand which slotted in behind the organ with a single metal rod giving a top platform, while on either side of the gilded apex strips of plywood hung down holding fourteen florette trays of floral foam covered with polythene, seven on each side (page 115). The arranging was done from above, behind the organ, and from the front on a gantry.

Beneath, at the west end of the entrance to the organ loft, was the unique construction for the beautiful archway of flowers. It measured 4 m (13 ft) to its top curve where, instead of meeting at the centre, the sides gently petered out leaving space for a fairly compact, frothy ball of carnations and gypsophila to hang in the centre.

The Royal Marines herald the bride with a fanfare of trumpets, and are complemented by the huge triangle of flowers in the organ loft

Flower ball, now complete, is ready to be hoisted to the correct position above the nave

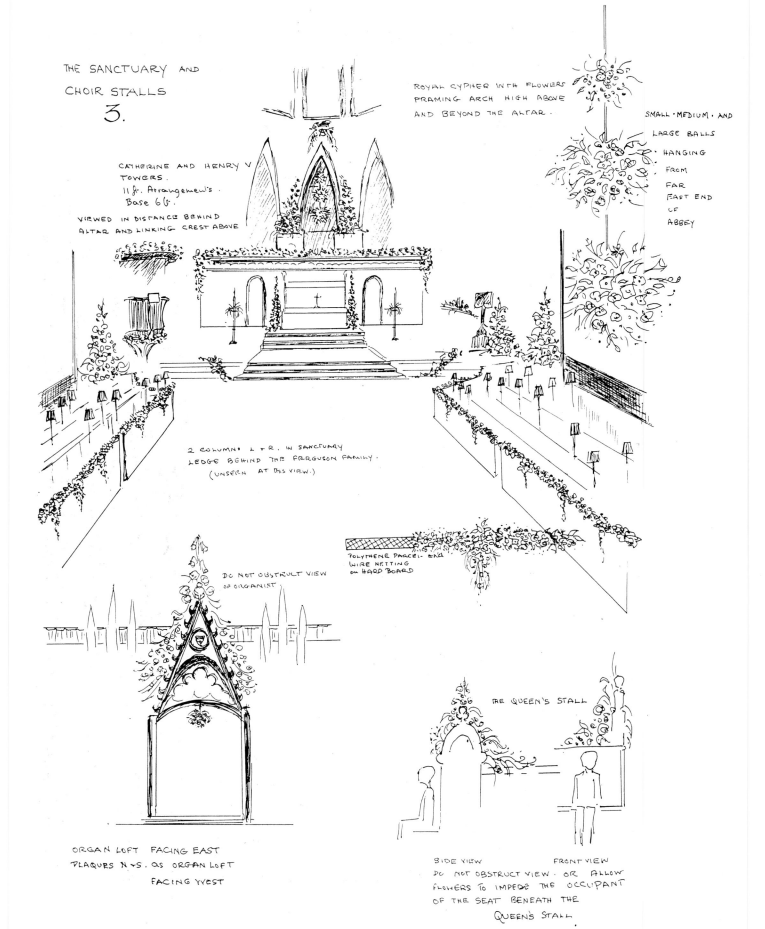

THE SANCTUARY AND
CHOIR STALLS
3.

ROYAL CYPHER WITH FLOWERS
FRAMING ARCH HIGH ABOVE
AND BEYOND THE ALTAR.

SMALL · MEDIUM · AND
LARGE BALLS
HANGING
FROM
FAR
EAST END
OF
ABBEY

CATHERINE AND HENRY V
TOWERS.
11 ft. Arrangements.
Base 6 ft.

VIEWED IN DISTANCE BEHIND
ALTAR AND LINKING CREST ABOVE

2 COLUMNS L + R. IN SANCTUARY
LEDGE BEHIND THE FERGUSON FAMILY.
(UNSEEN AT THIS VIEW.)

POLYTHENE PARCEL· BAG
WIRE NETTING
ON HARD BOARD

DO NOT OBSTRUCT VIEW
OF ORGANIST

ORGAN LOFT FACING EAST
PLAQUES N + S. AS ORGAN LOFT
FACING WEST

THE QUEEN'S STALL

SIDE VIEW   FRONT VIEW
DO NOT OBSTRUCT VIEW. OR ALLOW
FLOWERS TO IMPEDE THE OCCUPANT
OF THE SEAT BENEATH THE
QUEEN'S STALL

The bride and bridegroom process through the archway of flowers into the nave

The mechanics of the archway were as follows (page 113). A heavy, metal base held three outer rods and a smaller central one. The latter was removable and blocks of floral foam were threaded on to this like a giant necklace. Each side of the arch was in three parts which slotted into one another, polythene-covered floral foam fitted into the centre of the top curves and the whole was covered with wire netting. The arch fitted snugly into a corner of the moulding and was fixed at one point only, 3 m (9 ft) up where there was a space in the stonework through which a wire, well-cushioned with foam, was tied. From a distance this did not show, but the safety factor was ensured. The decoration proved to be a long and arduous task for the arrangers who, working on a gantry from the top meticulously down to the bottom, took one and a half days to complete it.

The two balls which hung within this archway were a pair of 30.5 cm (12 in) diameter plastic-coated, hanging flower baskets joined together. Heads of pale pink and cream carnations covered the surface, with stems only 7.5–10 cm (3–4 in) long, and the whole was covered with a froth of gypsophila (page 113).

The tops of the choir stalls were lined with lengths of wood backed with foam to protect the woodwork, carrying a continuous line of floral foam covered with polythene and wire netting which turned the corner at the easterly ends bordering the stalls. Florette containers were hung at intervals to give a 'bouquet' effect. Large quantities of cupressus and alchemilla were used as a base for rosebuds, spray carnations, chrysanthemums, freesias and 'Blushing Bride' proteas. White heather, brought especially from Scotland for good luck, was tucked into the completed borders of flowers (page 115).

On the day we walked round the Abbey, the Prince, noticing the pulpit, said: 'How lovely to have flowers up there...and along the top of the altar'. I looked dubiously at the Abbey officials, fearing their concern for the fabric of both, but following their approval and with great care we circled the top of the pulpit with flowers in shallow containers. This circle was matched by a smaller one around the base of the pulpit. The top arrangement showed well above the heads of the guests on many camera shots and the lower ring complemented it beautifully, but did not obscure the view of the guests who sat in the north transept.

Surprisingly, the top of the altar screen was 1 m (4 ft) wide, but it had a sheer drop of a least 4.5 m (15 ft) on each side. The border of flowers, with a huge central bouquet of longiflorum lilies, was the background for the wedding ceremony and was no small achievement for the arranger. The flowers were arranged in guttering 6 m (20 ft) long (page 116).

Somewhat precarious feats of flower arranging took place in the north and south transepts, where it was essential to have flowers visible for the pleasure of the many royal guests and foreign dignitaries. The graded arrangements sited on narrow shelves 46 cm (18 in) wide and 6 m (20 ft) above the transepts were spectacular but, sadly, they did not appear in any published photographs (pages 116–17).

The chancel steps were bordered by flowers arranged in three containers, which flowed from step to step, and there were many delightful

The soft glow of the candlelamps enhanced the beauty of the flowers, and their warmth increased the scent of the lilies and roses which were tucked into these borders

A view taken from the north transept looking back through the choir towards the organ loft

The altar, now adorned with the ceremonial
cream and gold frontal in readiness for the
wedding. The large triangular plaque with the
Royal Cypher and three graded flower balls
hanging below it are seen at the most easterly
end of the Abbey. The tips of the sixteen-feet
high arrangements described on page 122 may
be seen behind the altar screen

*The graded arrangements in the north transept
with a central plaque containing the Royal
Cypher*

117

NORTH TRANSEPT.

4.

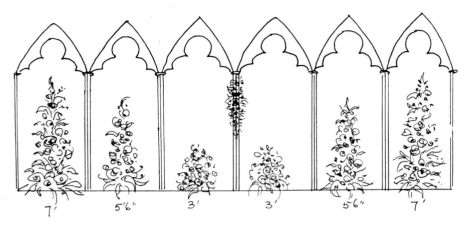

7'   5'6"   3'   3'   5'6"   7'

HEIGHT OF ALCOVE 7'6"
WIDTH   "   "   3'10"
DEPTH   "   "   3'8"

PLAQUE WITH ROYAL CYPHER ATTACHED TO
CENTRE PILLAR.

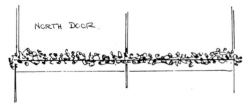

NORTH DOOR.

SOUTH TRANSEPT

PLAQUE WITH ROYAL
CYPHER ATTACHED
TO CENTRE PILLAR.

St. EDWARD'S CHAPEL.

THE REGISTER WILL BE SIGNED HERE.

EDWARD I TOMB

THIS ARRANGEMENT TO FACE 3 SIDES.

35. ARRANGEMENT ON ALTAR.
36 ARRANGEMENT EITHER SIDE
     OF CORONATION CHAIR
37 'SPECIAL' ON TABLE

38 BOOKMARK.

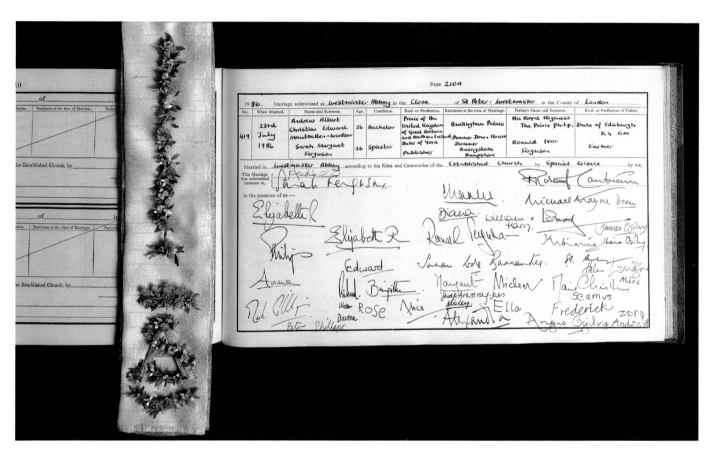

Bookmark on the register

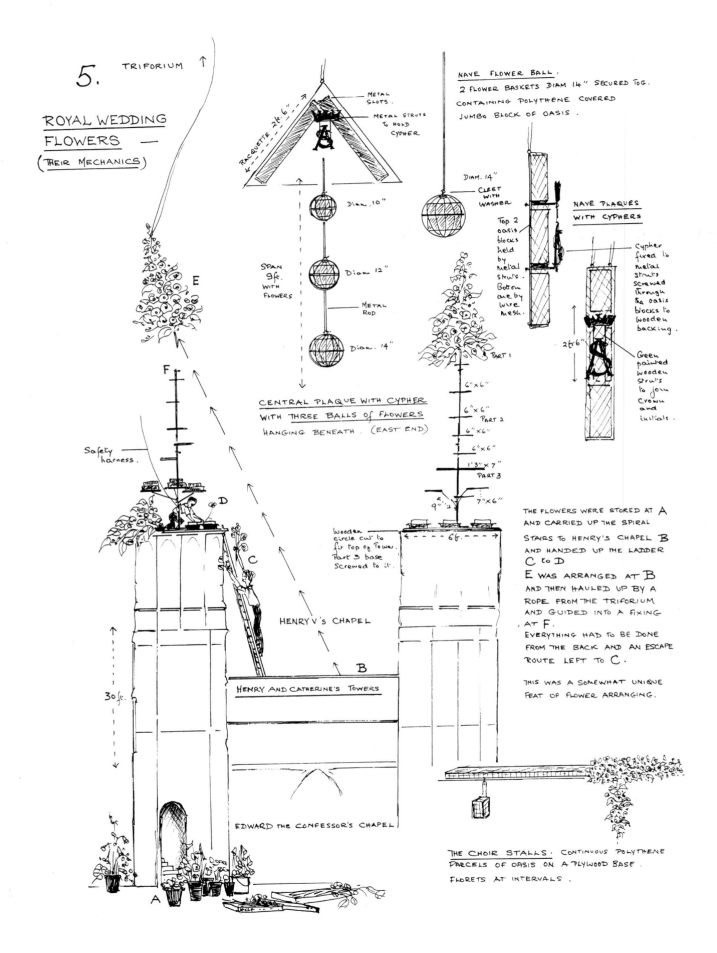

5.

ROYAL WEDDING
FLOWERS —
(THEIR MECHANICS)

TRIFORIUM ↑

Racquette 2ft.6"

METAL SLOTS.
METAL STRUTS TO HOLD CYPHER

Diam. 10"

SPAN 9ft. WITH FLOWERS

Diam. 12"

METAL ROD

Diam. 14"

CENTRAL PLAQUE WITH CYPHER
WITH THREE BALLS OF FLOWERS
HANGING BENEATH. (EAST END)

NAVE FLOWER BALL.
2 FLOWER BASKETS DIAM 14" SECURED TOG.
CONTAINING POLYTHENE COVERED
JUMBO BLOCK OF OASIS.

Diam. 14"
CLEET WITH WASHER

Top 2 oasis blocks held by metal struts. Bottom one by wire mesh.

NAVE PLAQUES WITH CYPHERS

Cypher fixed to metal struts screwed through the oasis blocks to wooden backing.

2ft.6"

Green painted wooden struts to join Crown and initials.

E

F

Safety harness.

D

C

Wooden circle cut to fit top of Tower. Part 3 base Screwed to it.

HENRY V's CHAPEL

PART 1

6"x6"

6"x6" Part 2

6"x6"

6"x6"

1'3"x7" PART 3

7"x6"

9"...

— 6 ft. —

30 ft.

B

HENRY AND CATHERINE'S TOWERS

EDWARD THE CONFESSOR'S CHAPEL

A

THE FLOWERS WERE STORED AT A
AND CARRIED UP THE SPIRAL
STAIRS TO HENRY'S CHAPEL B
AND HANDED UP THE LADDER
C to D
E WAS ARRANGED AT B
AND THEN HAULED UP BY A
ROPE FROM THE TRIFORIUM
AND GUIDED INTO A FIXING
AT F.
EVERYTHING HAD TO BE DONE
FROM THE BACK AND AN ESCAPE
ROUTE LEFT TO C.

THIS WAS A SOMEWHAT UNIQUE
FEAT OF FLOWER ARRANGING.

THE CHOIR STALLS. CONTINUOUS POLYTHENE
PARCELS OF OASIS ON A PLYWOOD BASE.
FLORETS AT INTERVALS.

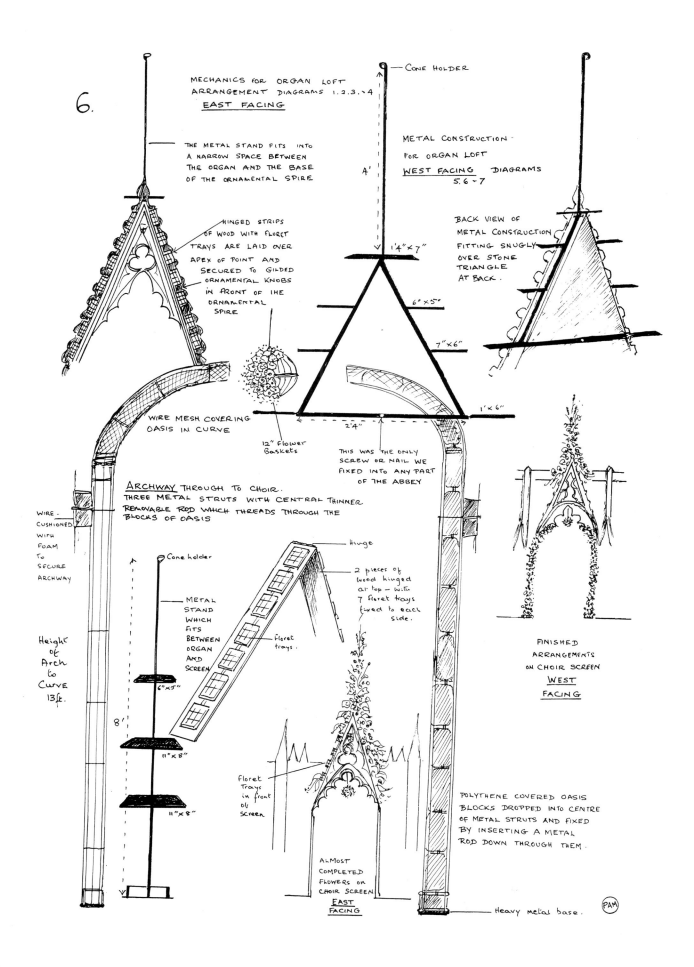

6.

MECHANICS FOR ORGAN LOFT
ARRANGEMENT DIAGRAMS 1. 2. 3. & 4
EAST FACING

THE METAL STAND FITS INTO
A NARROW SPACE BETWEEN
THE ORGAN AND THE BASE
OF THE ORNAMENTAL SPIRE

HINGED STRIPS
OF WOOD WITH FLORET
TRAYS ARE LAID OVER
APEX OF POINT AND
SECURED TO GILDED
ORNAMENTAL KNOBS
IN FRONT OF THE
ORNAMENTAL
SPIRE

WIRE MESH COVERING
OASIS IN CURVE

12" FLOWER
Baskets

— Cone Holder

METAL CONSTRUCTION
FOR ORGAN LOFT
WEST FACING DIAGRAMS
5. 6 ~ 7

BACK VIEW OF
METAL CONSTRUCTION
FITTING SNUGLY
OVER STONE
TRIANGLE
AT BACK.

A'

1'4" × 7"

6" × 5"

7" × 6"

1' × 6"

2'4"

THIS WAS THE ONLY
SCREW OR NAIL WE
FIXED INTO ANY PART
OF THE ABBEY

ARCHWAY THROUGH TO CHOIR.
THREE METAL STRUTS WITH CENTRAL THINNER
REMOVABLE ROD WHICH THREADS THROUGH THE
BLOCKS OF OASIS

WIRE
CUSHIONED
WITH
FOAM
TO
SECURE
ARCHWAY

Height
of
Arch
to
Curve
13 ft.

8'

Cone holder

METAL
STAND
WHICH
FITS
BETWEEN
ORGAN
AND
SCREEN

6" × 5"

11" × 8"

11" × 8"

— Hinge

2 pieces of
wood hinged
at top — with
7 floret trays
fixed to each
side.

Floret
trays.

Floret
Trays
in front
of
Screen

ALMOST
COMPLETED
FLOWERS ON
CHOIR SCREEN
**EAST
FACING**

FINISHED
ARRANGEMENTS
ON CHOIR SCREEN
**WEST
FACING**

POLYTHENE COVERED OASIS
BLOCKS DROPPED INTO CENTRE
OF METAL STRUTS AND FIXED
BY INSERTING A METAL
ROD DOWN THROUGH THEM.

— Heavy metal base.

(PAM)

photographs of the pages and bridesmaids sitting amongst them. The flowers in the chancel and by the altar had to be planned very carefully because of the large number of people present. A narrow ledge on an ancient tomb behind the Ferguson family was filled with flowers, and beautiful orchids which had been sent by the orchid farm in Jersey were arranged behind the Royal family. These were flanked by the magnificent Abbey gold plate which is displayed on special occasions.

It was essential that the two altar columns should be tall and tailored and should in no way protrude into the already narrow doorways either side through which the bride, bridegroom and members of their families would pass when they processed into St Edward's Chapel to sign the register. It had been a source of concern to the Prince and his bride-to-be as to whether her dress would flow through these doors. Indeed, it was understood that His Royal Highness had marked out the equivalent space at Buckingham Palace where they had practised, thus ensuring that he and his new Duchess would emerge from the chapel with ease.

The Chapel of Edward the Confessor, sited immediately behind the great, gilded altar screen, the very heart of Westminster Abbey, was decorated with a few special arrangements for the signing of the register. A dainty arrangement of garden flowers by the Founder President of NAFAS was placed on the table with the register. A bookmark of tiny silk flowers with the cypher in gold brocade, as described on page 134, was laid on the register. After the ceremony it was presented to the bride and bridegroom at our request.

As a finale for the design the two great towers of Henry V's Chancery Chapel rising 9 m (30 ft) from the ambulatory inspired the most ambitious scheme, but this presented problems that seemed insurmountable. The Clerk of Works pointed out that the stonework could be damaged and that it wouldn't be safe for the arrangers at that height. Even he did not know what the tops of the towers were like! So we climbed the 180 steps to the triforium, looked down to see for ourselves and then went home to think. The Henry V Tower contained a spiral staircase with steps so well worn that one's mind boggled at the thought of the numbers of people who must have climbed them through the centuries. They led up into Henry's private chapel, a tiny, plain stone room with an altar and railings overlooking Edward the Confessor's shrine. Flowers on top of these towers and hanging from the most easterly and highest point of the triforium would be the culmination of the plans for the Royal Wedding.

After several weeks of detailed planning, two stands were made in three parts. The lower sections were screwed to chipboard bases made to fit the uneven tops of the towers (diameter 2 m (6 ft) and these sections each had three movable metal shelves on a central rod which could be revolved and put into place once the arrangements were complete. The middle section with five platforms was slotted into the lower one, whilst the top one, which had four shelves and a holder at the top for a cone, was completed on the stone floor of the chapel then raised by a rope, swung into position and guided into its fixing in the middle section. By now the arranger, with a builder's safety harness securing him to a beam, was working in the

The bride and bridegroom process towards the West Door

centre of his column and had to leave an escape route in the back through which to reach his ladder. Large washing-up bowls round the front edge of the circle allowed plant material to flow over the rim. The finished pair of columns, at least 5 m (16 ft) high, were a feat of engineering and mountaineering coupled with skilful flower arranging, and were certainly worth all the anxieties, heartaches and doubts.

Beyond and above these towers hung a huge plaque in the centre of the triforium. It was formed on a triangular piece of chipboard with metal slots to hold two racquettes (90 cm (3 ft) long, solid lines of floral foam in a plastic base) angled from the apex, and a metal rod, similar to those in the nave, held the largest royal cypher. Below it were suspended three graded balls of flowers in 25.5 cm (10 in), 30.5 cm (12 in) and 35.5 cm (14 in) diameter containers constructed, as before, from hanging baskets joined together and supported by a central, metal rod. The overall span was 3 m (9 ft) and the total weight approximately 50 kg (110 lbs). Thus, on entering the Abbey through the west doors, the theme of the royal cypher, the entwined 'A' and 'S' surmounted by the crown, was carried through the nave and transepts to this most easterly and highest point in the Abbey.

Surely I had fulfilled my brief for flowers to be high and clearly visible to the congregation and to the cameras. It was an experience which I shall never forget, especially the moment when I walked through the Abbey and saw that all our ideas had come to life and here, indeed, was a setting fit for this great occasion. As the security guards and sniffer dogs came in at 7.00pm I took a bunch of yellow roses from a bucket in our flower store and arranged them casually in an Abbey container. I placed them on the table in St Edmund's Chapel, which had been prepared with mirror, brush and comb for the bridegroom and his best man who would be waiting there for the arrival of the bride. Way back in April Miss Ferguson had told me that yellow roses were the Prince's favourite flowers.

CHAPTER NINE

Bridal bouquets

David Longman

drop bouquet

A BRIDE has been described as a 'princess for a day', an appellation which applies to her appearance and bearing. Great care must be given to her selection of dress and the flowers which she will carry, for the two are very much complementary and neither should overshadow the other. Once the dress has been chosen, careful consideration must be given to the flowers and the way in which they should be arranged. One might well wonder why a bride carries flowers at all.

Flowers are essentially an expression of emotion: of love, of devotion and of sympathy. They feature at any important event in the progress of man through life: birth, marriage, anniversaries and death. They are provided at private occasions, at corporate functions, in business and in pleasure. They often convey sentiments that the ordinary man and woman cannot express themselves.

So why does a bride carry flowers? If we look back in history to the times of the Stuarts, we can see that nosegays of sweet-smelling flowers and herbs were carried by the gentry to ward off the plague and unpleasant odours due to bad drainage and lack of attention to personal hygiene. Such posies were carried on all formal occasions and weddings may well be considered one. Traditionally, similar posies are carried today by the Aldermen of the City of London and by High Court judges at the opening of sessions. The posy carried by the Queen on Maundy Thursday is made up of a special recipe of flowers and is provided by the holder of the appointment of Royal Nosegay Maker to the Queen. It was originally carried to protect the monarch from the odours of the poor whilst he/she washed their feet and distributed gifts of money. Needless to say, the practice of washing feet has long since been discontinued but special Maundy money – one coin for each year of the sovereign's life – is still distributed and the Maundy posies are still made during the night before the service.

However, I would like to think in more romantic terms and see the bouquet carried by the bride as the first token of love and affection given to her by her husband on their wedding day which, in return, she carries to the altar to show that she returns his love. This is why, at the end of the feast, she throws her bouquet into the crowd of wellwishers as she departs so that, supposedly, somebody else can share her good fortune.

Let us now consider the various types of bouquet that are available and what can be created to complement the bridal gown. There are three basic designs for bouquets and from those come many variations. Firstly, the drop bouquet, sometimes called shower or pear shape, which consists of a dominant flower surrounded by supporting flowers. It produces an almost fan-like shape at the top narrowing down below the focal point to a drop section which is usually as long, if not longer, than the main body of the bouquet. This is easily the most popular design. It can be executed in either a mixture of delicate flowers or with just one type of flower such as lilies, roses or orchids. The second shape is the crescent or, more often, the half crescent where the bouquet is held very much in the middle. Again, the central flowers are dominant with the two tails being of equal length in the full crescent, whilst in the half, the lower tail is usually longer. This is a style which often suits, if I dare say it, the less slender bride. Finally, there is the dainty, all-round posy, always popular especially for the slightly less formal dress. This, again, can take various forms: the strict, Victorian posy with its formal circles of contrasting colours; or the loose design of mixed, dainty flowers in either self or mixed colours.

Bridal bouquets should always reflect the style of the dress. Elaborate, flowing dresses require large, flowing bouquets and more tailored dresses need a bouquet that is long and slender. Short dresses or suits require slightly different treatment, although the three basic designs still apply. These bouquets should be very much smaller and I would strongly advocate the use of only one or two types of flowers.

Bridesmaids' bouquets, especially for adults, should always mirror the bride's, except that they should be about two thirds of the size. If there are two colours in the bride's bouquet one will always predominate and this colour pattern can often be reversed to great effect in the bridesmaids' bouquets. Child bridesmaids require completely different treatment. Miniature versions of the bride's bouquet can look out of place in the hands of a child and so often they carry them the wrong way up which completely spoils the whole picture. A small, round posy with a little, natural frill of dainty foliage can look charming. Other suggestions are floral balls held by a piece of ribbon, country or garden baskets with a hooped handle or, if it is a winter wedding, part or complete floral muffs. If the bridesmaids are very young the flowers should not only be simple but robust – young children quickly become bored and the flowers they are holding can get damaged.

Headdresses of natural flowers, both for brides and bridesmaids, are becoming very fashionable. I love to see them as complete circlets of flowers with relatively large flowers in the centre, rather like a tiara in shape. They should be made on a flexible wire, firmly fixed to the hair, as, if

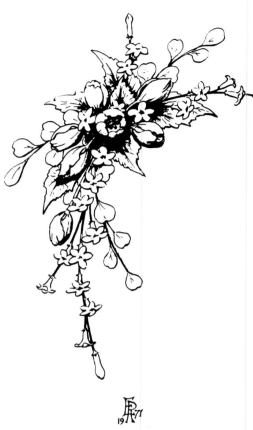

Curved bouquet

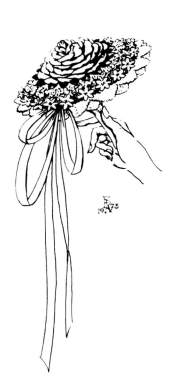

Bridesmaid's posies

too large, they can slip over the brow to look rather like a floral sunshade. A floral spray across the back of the head is also very becoming.

It is important to remember that an overall picture is being created. The focal point is the bride supported by her bridesmaids and maids of honour, so not only the dresses but the flowers, too, must be linked and co-ordinated. In this way, the bride will look and be 'princess for a day'.

Royal bouquets

One of the ancient livery companies of the City of London is the Worshipful Company of Gardeners and its existence can be traced back to 1345. It has the privilege of presenting the Royal family with bouquets of flowers on all important occasions: wedding days, state occasions such as coronations and jubilees, and all special anniversaries.

My family has had the honour of holding the appointment of Master of this Company since my father, Martin Longman, was requested to prepare the wedding bouquet for the then Princess Elizabeth in 1947. He was, at that time, invited to Buckingham Palace to discuss her wishes, following which he prepared sketches of various designs. From these the Princess selected the magnificent bouquet of orchids which he delivered personally on the morning of the wedding. When he arrived at Buckingham Palace, he was asked to incorporate a piece of myrtle from a bush at Osborne House, which had grown from a sprig that had been in Queen Victoria's wedding bouquet.

In 1960 we were honoured to receive another call, this time from Princess Margaret. She asked for a simple, half-crescent shaped bouquet of white flowers. Mindful of the hay fever from which Lord Snowdon suffered, these flowers were chosen with great care and strongly scented flowers avoided.

The Duke and Duchess of Kent were married in 1961 in York Minster, and the future Duchess requested a bouquet of white roses and orange blossom. The latter was not an easy flower to get in quantity and quality and this bouquet had to be made late at night in order to reach Hoveringham Hall on time. This was before the days of fast motorways and even at night the old A1 was a slow and tedious road on which to travel.

Two years later Princess Alexandra was married to Mr Angus Ogilvy in Westminster Abbey. She insisted on having white narcissi in her charming all-round posy, which was certainly not the ideal flower for a wedding bouquet, and it had to be made up at the last possible moment before the wedding. The bridesmaids, who included Princess Anne, carried miniature replicas of the bride's flowers.

Seventeen years passed before the next Royal Wedding, when the Prince of Wales married Lady Diana Spencer in St Paul's Cathedral. I had several meetings with the future Princess of Wales; sketches were made and sample bouquets prepared for discussion and for her choice. She was delighted with the result as, indeed, were we, for the final bouquet which measured 1.2 m (4 ft) from end to end included magnificent orchids, lily of the valley, gardenias, stephanotis, carnations and, at her special request, the yellow 'Mountbatten' roses. We made two bouquets, one for the service and the second for the photographs, each taking five girls four

hours to make. The size had a dramatic effect on the fashion for wedding bouquets for they had been getting smaller and smaller and now, suddenly, everybody wanted larger bouquets again, not always as large as Princess Diana's but certainly flowing and beautiful arrangements rather than three flowers and an ivy leaf!

In 1986 we made the wedding bouquet for Miss Sarah Ferguson. Breaking with tradition, Miss Ferguson requested a floral 'S' made up of lilies, roses, gardenia, lily of the valley and a sprig of myrtle, which she carried down the aisle of Westminster Abbey, setting a new trend in 'initial' bouquets. This was designed in association with Jane Packer, who advised the now Duchess of York on her bridal flowers and those of her retinue.

One charming gesture occurred in 1923 when the Queen Mother, Lady Elizabeth Bowes Lyon, married the then Duke of York (later to become King George VI). After the service in Westminster Abbey, a most splended, glittering occasion and the first 'Royal Event' after the Great War, the Duchess laid her wedding bouquet on the tomb of the unknown warrior. Since that time, although not always in person, every royal bride has followed this tradition.

H.R.H. *the Duchess of York's bouquet*

Bouquet, bridesmaid's basket and wreath. Made by Brian Howard, Marley Flowers, Haslemere

CHAPTER TEN

Happy memories

NEITHER THE bride nor bridegroom nor, indeed, any of the guests, should be impatient with the wedding photographer. He has a difficult task at the best of times, having been commissioned to photograph various family groups in order to record the 'great day' and capture the moment as nothing else can. If the photographs are bad he will be blamed and they cannot be retaken. So he must struggle against all the odds of the sun going behind a cloud, a sudden rainstorm, wind swooping up the bride's veil (or, worse, the mother-in-law's skirt) and he must shepherd the relations, bridesmaids and best man in and out of groups as required. All the time he knows that the guests, still trapped in the church, are longing to progress to the next stage of the proceedings – the champagne!

Photographs are forever

It is, of course, preferable if the guests can trickle out of side doors and stand around in warm sunshine, meeting friends and watching the photography with sympathetic tolerance. They must appreciate the importance of the photographic efforts to capture the magic of the day for future generations for, in later years, the pages of this album will be turned and someone will say, 'This was granny and grandpa's wedding'.

Video cameras are becoming more and more popular, and many brides employ a professional to record the event as well. Others have friends who offer to bring their cameras and, although this may result in a series of breathtaking 'pans' sweeping over the guests at high speed, they can produce something to look back on with varying degrees of pleasure. Certainly, it is the photographs that provide us with our most tangible memories, but flowers, too, have their part as keepsakes.

Bridal plaques

The wedding plaque worked by Beryl Greenslade has already been photographed in our village hall wedding (page 66). This can serve the dual purpose of providing a delightful decoration for a buffet table and then a keepsake for the bride and groom.

Wedding plaque

(1) The oval base was covered in peach dupion material, edged with peach braid and backed with felt, to which a ribbon hanger was fixed.

(2) A smaller oval was cut in lightweight card covered in cream dupion and edged with a narrow, cream braid. This was fixed to the larger oval base.

(3) The frame between the two ovals was decorated with long-grain rice and lentils, lacquered with two pale shades of pearly nail varnish and glued in a zigzag. Each zigzag was linked top and bottom with anaphalis flowerheads.

(4) Two heart shapes were cut in card and covered with the cream material and two outlines of hearts of similar size were cut and covered in peach material. Each heart was then decorated with diagonal strips of peach ribbon, in between which were glued sea lavender flowers alternating with seed tapioca painted with pearl nail varnish, thus resembling seed pearls. The hearts were then glued to the base, slightly overlapping, and the heart outlines attached to their outer edges, one having been cut to allow them to be interlocked.

(5) The initials of the bride and bridegroom were then lightly drawn in pencil above and below the hearts and were decorated with anaphalis flowerheads sprayed bronze and centred with lentils lacquered with pearl nail varnish.

(6) The wedding date was worked in seed tapioca painted with the same nail varnish.

(7) The two spray arrangements curving round each side of the inner plaque contained various dried and glycerined plant material including glixia, strawflowers, ferns, grevillia, helichrysum buds, miniature poppy seed heads and various grasses.

(8) The plaque was finished with peach and cream ribbon bows and tails fixed to the lower edge of the inner oval.

Flowers preserved in domes

In the first chapter I mentioned that the custom of the bride tossing her bouquet to the bridesmaids as she goes away is becoming much less popular. If the bridesmaid is disappointed, for tradition says that if she catches the bouquet she will be the next to marry, there is nevertheless a very good reason for deflecting it elsewhere. There may be a flower-arranging friend amongst the guests eager to catch the bouquet, with the thought of preserving it for the bride as a nostalgic reminder of her wedding day. The flowers from a bridal bouquet or the flowers which decorated the top of the wedding cake can be dried and arranged in containers under glass domes (see the photograph overleaf).

On the left, the arrangement contains a variety of flowers and foliage taken from a bouquet, e.g., orchids, rosebuds, freesias, white heather and tiny trails of ivy and asparagus fern. The base of the dome is covered in the cream silk of the bridal dress and the container is a small, glass urn which had been used for the cake top.

On the right, in a slightly smaller dome, the flowers and foliage include the sprays of pearls which had been part of the bouquet.

In the third and smallest dome the foliage and flowers, once dried, were sprayed with gold paint giving the effect of a metal sculpture of flowers. This can be quite an effective memento for it can be re-sprayed from time to time and there is, of course, no risk of the flowers fading in colour.

Preserving the flowers from a bouquet is not quite as straight-forward as drying those picked from the garden on a sunny day and dried immediately. They will, of course, have been handled by the florist in the first place and then will have spent part of the wedding day waiting for the bride to carry them to church; they will have been transferred back and forth to the bridesmaid and, finally, been left lying beside the cake during the reception. However, the chances are that a sufficient quantity will dry satisfactorily to provide a lasting arrangement as a keepsake. The method is as follows:

1. Flowers should be wired before drying since they will be too brittle to handle afterwards. This will make them easier to arrange.

2. A deep, airtight container should be used – a rigid, polythene sandwich box is ideal.

3. Pour the drying substance into the container to a depth of approximately 1.3 cm ($\frac{1}{2}$ in). A variety of preservatives are available and may be used, *e.g.*, borax, alum, silver sand or silica gel.

4. Place the flowers individually, not overlapping, across the surface of the preservative and gently sprinkle more preservative over them until they are completely covered.

5. A second or third layer of flowers, leaves, etc., may be added depending on the depth of the container; ensure that each petal of every flower is always covered with the powder or crystals.

6. Place the lid on the container and seal with clear adhesive tape or, if there is no lid, cover with several layers of clingfilm taped round the edge. Put in a dry place and leave for three to five days (larger flowers may need longer).

7. When removing the flowers from the preservative handle them with great care and shake all traces of powder from them (a soft paintbrush can help this process). Lay the flowers carefully on tissue paper before arranging.

The preservative can be used again if kept in a warm place and dried thoroughly each time before use. The drying process can be speeded up if the container with the flowers and preservative is well covered and placed for $2^1/_2$ minutes in a microwave oven on medium heat – but remember that containers suitable for microwaves must be used. It would be wise to experiment with similar flowers before using those from the bouquet.

Individual pressed flower creations

The second method of preserving the flowers from a bridal bouquet, now increasing in popularity, is by pressing them and making a picture. We are fortunate in having here Anne Plowden's expert account of this process.

Pressing and framing a wedding bouquet as a romantic reminder of that most special of days has its roots in the Victorian era. It was the Victorians who really introduced the romance of flowers into their gardens and who filled their houses with floral motifs on china, glass, wallpaper and furnishings. They even decorated their water closets and wash basins with flowery designs! It was considered a harmless and desirable occupation to go out into the garden and country lanes collecting flowers, leaves and mosses to bring back for identification and pressing, and the well brought-up, young Victorian lady was, of course, expected to supply the correct botanical names in Latin!

Methods of pressing flowers have not changed in essence since those days, although now flowers are first placed on blotting paper before being put in a book with really absorbent pages which is then slightly weighted.

It is interesting to note that wedding bouquets are made up of very much the same sort of flowers as 140 years ago, although there would have been more seasonal variation then. Roses and lily of the valley have always been firm favourites, representing, as they do, love and happiness. In fact, Victorians were expert at communicating through the language of flowers, sending little posies which would speak volumes — not always romantic nonsense but sometimes quite astringent comments! To the Victorians red carnations said 'alas, my poor heart' to the recipient and, indeed, they have always been associated with romance.

Hothouse flowers such as stephanotis, Alstroemeria ligtu hybrids, chincherinchees and all the orchids press beautifully; the cymbidium orchid, exceptionally, undergoes a dramatic transformation in pressing and comes out a rich brown. Colours deepen during pressing and so a pale pink rose will become warm pink, white flowers turn to cream and scarlets to dark red. The only blue flowers to keep their colour are the delphinium, and its cousin the annual larkspur. There are still Victorian flower pictures in existence today with the blue of the delphinium virtually unchanged.

Gypsophila is a great delight as it gives such an airy look to the bouquet and, although the various ferns make a pretty contrast to the flowers, green leaves do gradually lose their colour or darken. Not so silver-grey leaves, such as artemisias, which always stay the same and look fresh and pretty in the finished picture. Of course, a little trail of ivy which speaks of 'fidelity in marriage' would be included in the bouquet.

It is unlikely that young ladies in the nineteenth century would have been encouraged to venture into the garden or countryside to pursue their gentle pastime of flower pressing if it were raining, thus they would never have discovered the disappointment that comes from trying to press wet flowers, because for a bright and colourful end result, they do need to be fresh, young and dry.

Wedding bouquets must be looked after carefully if they are to be pressed and the best method is to tuck soft, dry tissues in amongst the flowers to prevent them rubbing against each other, with more tissues above and below each flower. The whole parcel must then be put into a polythene bag and placed in the cool compartment of the refrigerator. Bouquets should never be put in a freezer or immersed in water.

The design of wedding bouquets has undergone many changes in relation to the fashion of the period, but the little Victorian posy is still a firm favourite for bridesmaids. Delightful holders, like little ice cream cones, were made in silver, often with beautifully intricate, chased designs; or there were simpler holders, made from glass, which would be supplied with the bouquet and returned to the florist for her next bride. These pre-date the modern equivalent in which the holders end with a ball of floral foam into which the flowers can be securely fixed, giving the florist the opportunity to create free-flowing, *unwired designs. The saddest period in the history of pressing wedding bouquets was in the middle of this century, when florists' wires caused blackened holes and pierced the heart of many a rose.*

Most flowers have to be pressed petal by petal, buds need to be treated separately from their thinner, fully-opened main flower and great care has to be taken to give each variety of flower the correct amount of pressing weight. The length of time varies with each type of flower and can last from six to ten weeks. Finally, all the individual petals have to be put back into their original shape, which in the case of chrysanthemums is quite a tricky process!

Recreating the shape of the bouquet, giving the impressions of colour, line, space and movement without the third dimension of depth is very much a matter of individual artistic interpretation and no two artists see things in the same way. Thus, the space available within the chosen frame dictates whether there is enough room, as in the photograph, for the whole effect to be freely expressed and the original shape of the bouquet reproduced, or whether just a few of the flowers can be displayed in a small frame. In that case the design does not attempt to capture the original shape of the bouquet, but is still a treasured memento.

The frame and colour background are very important and should be chosen first: the three elements of frame, background and flowers must complement each other. Dramatic effects can be achieved by using a dark background for pale flowers and softer, subtler effects by using a pale one. The completed picture should never be hung in direct sunlight or on a damp wall.

Pressed flower work is painstakingly slow and intricate, and patience and concentration are needed to 'see' and achieve the desired effect, which is probably why so many young ladies were encouraged to settle down in a quiet corner of the drawing room and employ themselves usefully under mama's watchful eye! Nonetheless, the end result is very personal and, in the case of a pressed wedding bouquet picture, has a special significance which underlines the Victorian adage that 'flowers are love's truest language'.

An example of an unusual keepsake is the delicate and intricately worked bookmark, skilfully made by Rosamond Wills, that is mentioned in the chapter on the Royal Wedding flowers. The design, in minute silk flowers, included the entwined 'A' and 'S' with the crown above in gold brocade, and is pictured on page 119.

Cherished memories are those not necessarily planned at the time but are ones which are appreciated over and over again through the years. When the pages of an album are turned, when a picture of pressed flowers is enjoyed, or when the sun shines through the dome of flowers, these perhaps provide the happiest memories, which help to enrich a relationship as the anniversaries go by.

They lived happily ever after

THE PREVIOUS pages have listed the wedding anniversaries and it is clear to see the type of gifts which may be expected to pass between husband and wife, or to be received by them from friends as the years go by. I remember attending a delightful tenth anniversary party when every guest brought a tin of food, varying from baked beans to salmon, and an extremely well-stocked larder resulted! It always seems to me to be a shame that one has to wait until one's sixtieth anniversary to enjoy a gift of diamonds for, even if one was married at 15 years of age, one would be 75 years old by then. Could we not exchange the seventh woollen anniversary for the diamond? At 75, or even 80 years old, there might be fewer opportunities for wearing precious stones, whereas 53 years earlier one could be guaranteed plenty of opportunities to wear diamonds with rather greater éclat!

ANNIVERSARIES

1st COTTON
2nd   Paper
3rd   Leather
4th   Fruit & Flowers

5th WOODEN
6th   Sugar
7th   Wool & Copper
8th   Bronze & Pottery
9th   Pottery & Willow

10th TIN
11th   Steel
12th   Silk & Linen
13th   Lace
14th   Ivory

15th CRYSTAL
20th   China

25th SILVER

30th PEARL
35th Coral

40th RUBY
45th Sapphire

55th EMERALD
60th DIAMOND
70th PLATINUM

50th GOLDEN

FOLIAGE

Arum italicum 'Pictum'
erica (heather)
Hedera helix 'Glacier' (ivy)
Hedera helix 'Marmorata Minor' (ivy)
Pittosporum tenuifolium 'Silver Queen'
Polypodium vulgare (wall fern)
Santolina chamaecyparissus (cotton
    lavender)
Senecio greyi

FLOWERS

10 white spray carnation (split up)
10 chrysanthemum 'Bonnie Jean'
        (split up)
15 petite white tulip

Silver

Although the illustration shows a husband and wife celebrating their silver wedding *à deux*, we chose to set a round table for a dinner party for six, and the guests enjoyed a quiet celebration of this couple's 25 years together.

The centrepiece was a Victorian epergne which had a base of four silver swans. There was a glass plate in the centre and an elaborate silver holder on the top held a glass funnel. The flowers were arranged on two levels and all the foliage used was grey. In front of each place setting a small dish with a 2.5 × 2.5 cm (1 × 1 in) piece of floral foam taped to it was arranged with a small posy of similar flowers.

Pearl

For the celebration of a pearl anniversary we made a very simple buffet arrangement. It was placed on two oval bases which were covered in cream dupion edged with pearl beading. The container is obtainable commercially and consists of two metal platforms joined by a metal hoop (mechanics no. 18). In this instance the hoop was covered with white and silver ribbon. Hanging beneath the top placement and attached round the platform were two pearl-covered wedding bells, particularly appropriate in this case, yet normally available as Christmas tree decorations.

FOLIAGE

Hedera helix 'Silver Queen' (ivy)
sprays of threaded pearls

FLOWERS

3 stems white spray carnations
1 stem 'White Spider' chrysanthemum
7 papaver seed heads sprayed (poppy)
10 *Rosa* 'Darling'
3 *Rosa* 'Jack Frost'

Silver Wedding;
dinner table

Pearl Wedding;
table centre

The arrangements contained the soft, pale pink 'Darling' roses, with glass baubles mounted on stub wires tucked in amongst the fresh plant material. The glass candleholders provided the party light for the table and their soft glow highlighted the pearl on the bells and the glass baubles amongst the flowers.

Ruby

Forty years – a ruby anniversary – and here the celebrations took place in one of the magnificent reception rooms at Fishmongers Hall in London. This arrangement, which included a pair of antique ruby-coloured glass oil lamps, was set on a beautiful pedestal table. The soft blue wall coverings and the deep ruby red, silk chair seat enhanced the display of flowers. Two heavy, round containers were used, one being raised on a velvet-covered plinth behind the lamps and the other towards the front on the circular base placed to protect the table top.

FOLIAGE	FLOWERS	
Arum italicum 'Pictum'	5	red carnation
Asparagus sprengeri	10	dark red spray carnation
Berberis julianae	20	red freesia
Eucalyptus gunnii (gum tree)	7	*Lilium* 'Stargazer'
Hebe 'Autumn Glory' (veronica)	10	red florist rose
Mahonia aquifolium		
Pinus lambertiana (sugar pine)		
Pittosporum tenuifolium 'Purpureum'		
Salix sachalinensis 'Setsuka'		

Gold

Finally, we set the golden wedding buffet table against the oak panelling in the Tudor Suite at Hever Castle. The soft, golden colours in the picture seemed the perfect centrepiece, and the flowers used complemented it well.

The S-shaped stands were wrought iron, painted gold and had two platforms for containers (mechanics no. 19).

FOLIAGE	FLOWERS	
cupressus	1	stem cream spray carnation (split up)
Euonymus fortunei radicans 'Emerald Charm'	3	dahlia double dwarf bedding
Foeniculum vulgare (fennel)	5	*Freesia* × *hybrida* 'Fantasy'
Hedera helix 'Buttercup' (ivy)	2	*Lilium* 'Mont Blanc'
Hosta fortunei 'Aurea Marginata' (plantain lily)	5	*Rosa* 'Golden Times'
Ligustrum ovalifolium 'Aureum' (privet)	3	cream *Matthiola* 'Brompton Strain' (stock)
Cotinus coggyria (Rhus, European smoke tree)		
Skimmia japonica		

The garlands along the front of the table were made using three small, polythene parcels which held golden roses, ribbon tails (mechanics no. 22) and lengths of *Asparagus asparagoides* (smilax) fixed with long dressmaking pins.

Ruby Wedding

I look forward to being asked to do the flowers for an emerald, a diamond or a platinum party. Doubtless, such events would warrant some splendid decorations. I would envisage all-green foliage arrangements and emerald ribbons for the emerald party, white flowers and sparkling ornaments for the diamond celebration (and, of course, gifts of diamonds for each guest); and platinum? I would have to think about that!

Golden Wedding

Index of flowers and foliage

General Index